# ✤A HORSE'S VOICE✤

## FIONA SUTTON

You stamp and throw your head up high.
As your mane cascades towards the sky.
Front legs dance above the ground,
Majestic animal I have found.

Soulful passion shines in your eyes,
The wind and air you do disguise,
In legs that thunder mercilessly,
Raining sparks delightfully.

You snort, your nostrils are alight,
On fire they flare throughout the night,
To light the way of your command
Hoof beats of time upon the sand.

Oh, great horse you cannot see,
Your beauty and your majesty,
I'm helpless! You have captured me,
Imprisoned my heart eternally.

God created you to cast His light,
To dispel the shadows that invade the night,
To give us hope in our darkest hour,
To revel in his greatest power.

FIONA SUTTON

*I dedicate this book
To the beautiful souls who live amongst us.
Whose only desire
Is for us to partner them
Kindly and compassionately,
Gifting them the respect and dignity
They so rightly deserve.
Is it so little to ask
From an animal who has served
Us so nobly and
Who has asked for so little in return?
When mankind has reached
A higher state of love,
Then and only then
Can we be considered
A partner worthy of The Horse.*

Copyright 2023 © Fiona Sutton. First published in the UK by Amazon. Fiona Sutton asserts the right to be identified as the author of this work. All rights reserved. No parts of this publication may be reproduced, stored in a retrieval system, or transmitted in any form, or by any means, electronic, mechanical, photocopying, recording or otherwise without the prior permission of the author.

This is a work of non-fiction. The events and experiences detailed herein are true and have been faithfully rendered as the author has remembered them as to the best of her ability.

**All the profits from the sale will go the Remus Memorial Horse Sanctuary**

# TABLE OF CONTENTS

| | |
|---|---|
| Acknowledgments | 5 |
| Author's Note to Text | 7 |
| Introduction | 8 |
| PART 1- THE JOURNEY | 10 |
| Chapter 1- The Horse Speaks | 10 |
| Chapter 2- My Questions Answered | 15 |
| Chapter 3- The Awakening | 22 |
| Chapter 4- Jazz's Story | 29 |
| PART 2- THE MULTI-FACETED HORSE | 44 |
| Chapter 5- The Spiritual Horse | 44 |
| Chapter 6- The Teaching Horse | 64 |
| Chapter 7- The Prey Horse | 86 |
| Chapter 8- The Training/Riding Horse | 103 |
| Chapter 9- The Sports/Competitive Horse | 134 |
| Chapter 10- The Psychic Horse | 142 |
| Chapter 11- The Abused Horse | 155 |
| Chapter 12- The Social Horse | 162 |
| Chapter 13- The Healing Horse | 176 |

| PART 3- DEEPER CONNECTION | 188 |
| --- | --- |
| Chapter 14- The Human Attitude | 188 |
| Afterword | 204 |
| The Unification Prayer | 206 |
| Epilogue | 207 |

# Acknowledgements

My deepest and sincerest gratitude goes to all those people who have supported me in writing this book. I am indebted to family and friends for their assistance in editing the book and their honest feedback.

I owe my reiki teacher, Helen Courtney, a big thank you for her massive support and encouragement on my spiritual path, empowering me to achieve things beyond my wildest dreams. It was her revelation that started me on the journey of writing this book. Her unwavering support and belief in me has enabled me to trust and have faith in something which just seemed impossible. Helen is a true earth angel, and I am so proud and grateful to be her student.

Another earth angel I am so grateful to is Jenny Smedley, renowned spiritual healer, author and artist, for the beautiful cover of my book. She has captured Jazz's spirit perfectly in her picture on the front cover, and I feel truly honoured that my book depicts her beautiful artwork.

A big thank you to my book coach, Katie Oman, who has helped me to edit and birth this book into the world. As a psychic, she's also the one who helped to start me off on this path through the guidance she gave me.

A big thank you must also go to my dad and my two children for encouraging me and helping in the editing of the book. I am also indebted to my husband for his unfailing support; made more notable by the fact that he does not share my spiritual beliefs.

A sincere and heartfelt thank you must also go to all those horse lovers out there, who are doing their utmost to create a better world for our wonderful equine partners. On our own we can do very little, but combined we can make a difference. There is no better time than now.

Thank you to everyone who has bought this book. Please lend this book to someone you know who will appreciate it. Even better, please buy them a copy, benefiting a horse charity in the process. It is important that the horse's message gets passed around. The profits from the sale of the book will go to the Remus Memorial Horse Sanctuary. I chose that charity because they use Animal Communication and reiki healing on their animals, and so they are very much aligned with the message in my book.

Last but not least, this book would never have been born if it wasn't for the wonderful horses who have graced my life. Tiffany is the one who set me on the spiritual path in the first place, with the many gifts she granted me on her transition, and Jazz my current horse has been the one who birthed this book. Not a day goes by when I am not filled with the utmost gratitude and joy for having her in my life and for being a channel for her voice to flow through me. I am beyond humbled to be a Voice for the Horse, and I hope the message will reach many people, helping them to see the horse in a different light. When we look at something through our soul eyes, the view is much changed, and in finding true, unconditional love for our horses, we will also find it for ourselves.

## AUTHOR'S NOTE TO TEXT

As horses are not inanimate objects and they do have gender, then in order to avoid using the pronoun "it" when referring to a horse, I have gone with convention and used "he."

I have also tried not to objectify animals by using the word "owner" when referring to the human side of an animal-human relationship. Instead, I use the term, the "animal's guardian."

I have also changed the names and identity of people and animals when it seems appropriate to do so.

# INTRODUCTION

By the time you are a few years away from celebrating your half century on Earth, you feel you have a good grasp on life. You have been around long enough to understand the way things work and how people think and act. In short, you feel you know and understand reality.

But then, something happens, and your illusion is shattered. You realise that the story you had made up about reality, is just that, a story. It is no more real than the dreams you escape to at night. Like a child that is new to the world, you start looking at the world with very different eyes. As your whole perception, beliefs and thinking changes, you start creating a very different reality for yourself. This process is termed "An Awakening." I know this is for real, because it happened to me. And it transformed my life.

As a result of that awakening, I walked a very different path to before. In search for answers, I became fascinated with all things spiritual. It was inevitable that my journey was entwined with that of the horse. After all, it was the horses who had brought me to this place. It was the horses who had healed me and shown me a way out of the darkness. They are the ones who had drawn back the curtain, revealing a path to something way more magical. I owed them big time! This book is part of my promise to them. It is time their soul voice is heard.

It goes without saying that I have often asked, *"Why me?" Why have I been chosen to be a Voice for the horse?"* After all, in the words of one of the great Abba songs…

> *"I am nothing special, in fact I'm a bit of a bore. If I tell a joke, you probably have heard it before."*
>
> ~ Thank You for the Music

All those talents which would make someone an ideal candidate for the job are absent in me. I am not a writer, and my shy and retiring nature isn't a good requisite for someone to be an advocate for the horse. Nevertheless, I was chosen.

I now recognise that it isn't talents or abilities that helped win my role. I chose to open my mind and open my heart, and the very deep desire within me to help horses reared up in me. Like the phoenix rose from the ashes, it took on a life form all of its own. This yearning, deep from within the soul, was so pure and so egoless, that like a magnet, it drew towards it all the beautiful energies in the Universe. I was being supported!

Each and every one of us has the power within to be a Voice for the Horse. In fact, if things are to change, if we are to make a better world, not only for horses, but for ourselves, then we all need to stand up and be counted. We think it is impossible to make a difference, but this is just not true. When we stand together, then mountains can be moved. It is my greatest wish and hope that after reading this book, you too will find the power within yourself to stand up for those who can't defend themselves. The Horses need us. But more importantly, we need them!

# PART 1 – THE JOURNEY

## Chapter 1 – The Horse Speaks

*Horsemanship is like a holographic puzzle;*
*Having become fully au fait with its surface reality*
*You think you know it all.*
*Until one day a piece opens up*
*Revealing vast inner depths to be explored.*
*The search for answers has begun.*

The date 11/11/2016 was supposedly a magical day. In spiritual circles, the numbers 11:11 are considered hugely significant and powerful. These numbers are supposed to represent angelic presence and communication. So, the date 11/11/16 was supposed to be a day where the angels talk, and we can hear them. Well, if you consider a horse as an angel, then so it was. For that was the day my horse talked and spoke her truth.

In the few weeks leading up to that date, my horse Jazz had been trying to tell me something. It started with the words, *"This is all wrong. You are supposed to be using me for my mind not my body."* As I was leading her down to the ménage to ride, these words resounded in my head. There was no mistaking them, I could hear her loud and clear. This was a surprise to me, as although I am an Animal

Communicator, I don't normally hear things directly from the animals. Normally, it is necessary for me to go into a meditative trance, and I connect to the animal's energy from a photograph, enabling me to hear their soul voice. So, hearing my horse speak to me in this way was surprising to say the least.

Later in the day, when I arrived home, I did tune into my horse telepathically, asking her to explain what she had meant. In response to my plea to be a bit clearer, she expressed how she was a spiritual horse, and that she had come into my life to help and educate me. It was no accident that we had been brought together. Her task, she explained, was to lead me away from riding and training. She knew that my greatest wish was to truly understand horses and to help other people understand them. My purpose is as a healer, as is hers.

I reeled in shock from what I was hearing. Having spent the last 18 months trying to get her straighter, more supple and in much better physical shape, was I really prepared to throw it all away based on what I thought my horse was telling me? *"Ok,"* I told her, *"Please give me time to process what you are saying. I need this verifying. I need to know that what I am hearing is true. That it is not my mind making it up."*

Just two days later, the perfect opportunity arose. A lady who I had done an angel communication course with and who writes for a couple of the spiritual magazines, was asking on Facebook if anyone had an animal displaying a problem behaviour. She was going to read their aura (energy field), to see if she could get to the bottom of the problem. I decided to send her a picture of Jazz. I explained that she wasn't really enjoying her work at the moment – she was trying to nip when I put the bridle and saddle on, and sometimes she was planting and refusing to move in the ménage.

Her feedback completely confirmed what Jazz had been telling me. She explained that Jazz had a rainbow aura, which was very rare, and she was becoming increasingly aware of her spiritual nature. With this awareness, was the desire for me to acknowledge her special gifts. In particular, she wanted to be treated differently to the other horses.

Ok, so this was totally tying in with the information I was picking up. The next step was to find out exactly what I was supposed to be doing with this spiritual horse. Jazz was telling me she wanted to be a healer, but I just couldn't see how I could accommodate this wish. Although there are healing facilities abroad, there is nothing in this country. I realised I needed to get my Reiki teacher involved. I felt I was just too close to this – I needed someone who could talk to Jazz without the brain interference.

So, on 11/11/2016 my Reiki teacher came out and talked to my horse. Within seconds of walking into her stable, Jazz went into a deep trance, and remained that way for about 1 ½ hours (30 minutes after we had finished conversing with her). Despite everything I have witnessed and experienced, even I was shocked by what was to be revealed, for I had never heard anything like it before!

Jazz expressed her desire to form a healing partnership with myself. But before this, she wanted to co-write a book with me. This will be a book that will give a voice to the horse; a book that will show things from a horse's soul perspective; and will reveal how we can better partner the horse. As I reeled from this information, I was given a directive as to how this would happen. I would sit quietly in the stable with Jazz, pen and notebook in hand, and I would just allow the words to flow through. It would be exactly the same process as when I do Animal Communications for people – my conscious mind would be turned off, and the information would just flow through freely, without thinking about it. Eventually, it would become like automatic writing.

When I told my daughter, Lauren, about Jazz wanting to assist me with writing a book, she was standing outside Jazz's stable. *"That is absolutely crazy"* she stated matter-of-factly. The next moment, her face had turned to shock and disbelief. The words had no sooner popped out of her mouth, than Jazz glared at her, pinned her ears back flat against her head, shaking her head up and down, as if to say, *"How dare you mock me!"* That was telling her! Probably best that people keep their opinions to themselves. Jazz kept doing this, until eventually Lauren apologised to her, at which point she stopped.

The next day, I couldn't wait to start the book. With great anticipation, I moved a stool into Jazz's stable and sat there with an A4 book and pen. Jazz was relaxed, and unusually didn't even react when her stable mate, Silver, went on a ride. I meditated, connected with Jazz, and put my pen on the paper. I found myself listening to a voice in my head. Before I knew it, I had written a few pages, without a single pause and without my pen leaving the paper. Wow, this was for real! We really could do this! I was so excited. Magic doesn't even begin to describe it.

Two weeks later, my deeply sceptical daughter announced her conversion to the cause. She declared that she now believed 100%. I had written about 30 pages by then and every session had been the same. I would put my pen on the page, and it would just write itself; no pause, and no having to think what I was going to write. It just came to me.

However, the biggest change was in Jazz herself. Now that she had been heard and had been given a voice, all traces of grumpiness had just vanished. I had explained to her that she still needed to be exercised, as it was good for her to be kept fit and supple. But even though there was no change in her work routine, she was without doubt a totally different horse. Once again, this just proves that listening to our horses and considering their needs can create a deep shift in our relationship with them.

# CHAPTER 2 – MY QUESTIONS ANSWERED

*The horse gave up his freedom, to allow Man his.
There is no greater sacrifice.*

Not surprisingly, the first session with my horse was going to revolve around the many questions I had about writing this book. If I was to put my faith and belief in it, then Jazz would need to come up with some pretty convincing answers. As I sat in the stable, pen and A4 notebook in hand, I was preparing myself to ask the first question. But Jazz beat me to it.

**Jazz**: Thank you so much for taking this journey with me. It is a big leap of faith for anyone. Few people on being told that their horse wants to channel a book through them, would even be able to comprehend it, let alone give it a go. So, thank you for being open and willing to do this.

Deep down you always knew this was possible. When the horses healed you (see chapter 3) and you were in that bubble with them, you invited the opportunity in. Your very deep desire to help them be better understood was your soul calling; it was inevitable the Universe would assist, with such a pure and selfless intention. All the beautiful things that have happened since and chronicled in your first book, *Seeker of the Light*, have brought you to where you are today. All of the training you have undertaken, and the inner work you have carried out on yourself, has helped you reach a point where you can hear the soul voice of the horse. This has always been your deepest dream, so you are very much fulfilling your soul purpose.

The deep longing in your heart has been heard. This is the desire for humans and horses to form a true partnership, with each bringing their own unique sets of gifts and talents to the table; each recognising the brilliance and power in the other. When combined, it is a truly potent and powerful combination. In this togetherness, anything is possible. And now is the right time for this book.

**Me:** So why now? What do you mean by that?

**Jazz:** Times are changing. We are entering a new age, where the consciousness of the planet is rising. People's hearts and minds are opening. They are now ready to see horses in a new light.

Many hundreds of years ago, the horse/human partnership was more evolved than it is today. There was a time when humans revered and worshipped us – recognising and fully appreciating the massive benefits that an equal partnership would bring to them. The horse was valued higher than any other possession. But they also recognised the importance of developing a very close bond. If the horse was to be a willing worker and give their all, it was of vital importance that they were content and getting as much out of the partnership as the human. These tribal people took immense pride in their horses. There was competition amongst the people; not who had the fastest, or the best-looking horse, but who had the deepest relationship. From the moment the children were born, they were taught how to care for, love and respect the horse. These tribal people recognised an important truth: self-mastery, i.e., control of the inner self leads to mastery of others. They understood that through quieting the mind and obtaining complete stillness within, they had a much better chance of the horse reaching out and asking to partner them. They also recognised the importance of thinking like the horse. Through mimicking the horse's behaviour and their way of thinking, then minds would merge, enabling the horse to be completely compliant and obedient. When they rode, their bodies would be as one. No bridle or headpiece and no saddle. No whips or spurs; they were not required.

The rise of materialism and man's idolatry of the logical mind have given rise to the worst excesses of human nature. It has led to greed and egotistic thinking, resulting in separation, not only from each other, but from nature and the divine. But nothing is ever lost. A better union between man and horse is possible. Through this more equal partnership, it won't just be the horse who benefits; man will too. He will be led back, not only to nature, but to his true and authentic self; a state where he will find true happiness.

**Me:** Please tell me more about the human/horse relationship and how it came about.

**Jazz:** People think that in the beginning, it was man who captured the horse and used him for his own ends. But on the contrary, it was the horse who sought out and made the connection with man. For a prey animal, there would have been many benefits in forging such a partnership: food, shelter, protection, and even companionship. In return, the horse was happy to lend his gifts – strength, speed, ability to carry and move things, as well as the willingness to carry a rider. It was a mutually beneficial partnership.

Ultimately, however badly you have treated us, we will never give up on you. Yes, there have been times when you have treated us abominably – even systematically killing us for just being in your space- but the horse has been with you throughout your evolution and will never leave you. He will give you whatever you need, at that particular moment in your growth. He has offered his body for physical toil, but more and more of you are recognising he has even greater gifts to offer. The role of the horse is changing. Like a chameleon who changes to fit in with his environment, the horse changes to fit in with your evolution. By so doing, he is making himself indispensable.

The horse will always be with you. Even when man threatens to destroy the very planet he lives on, we will be there, attempting to lead you away from your worst excesses of violence and greed; trying to save you from yourselves. We are your chance for redemption.

**Me:** So, what is the book about and what is its aim?

**Jazz:** Hopefully, it will reveal the true nature of horses. Seen in this light, you will open up to the lessons that horses can teach you, and how they can help evolve your very souls. But in addition, you will be enlightened as to the many roles that horses take on. By the end of the book, the reader should have a much deeper understanding of how horses think and relate to the world, enabling them to forge a more unifying bond with horses. There will also be techniques included in the book, which will help facilitate this process, allowing man to relate to the horse at a soul level.

**Me:** What form will the book take?

**Jazz:** You just need to put your pen on the paper and follow the voice you hear in your head. It will be no different to when you carry out Animal Communications. You turn your brain off, and just allow the information to flow through, with no thought as to what is materialising. In the next chapter, you should tell your awakening story, as it is pivotal to everything that has followed. I will also tell my story, as it will help the reader to see things through the horse's eyes. The main body of the book will flow through you and the chapter headings will be obvious to you when you type it up. You will be given sub-headings and information will flow through pertaining to those topics.

But here is the important thing: this is to be a joint effort. When you type it up, you must include your own examples. Having spent forty years around horses, you have a great deal of understanding relating to their true nature, and you have been witness to many things. Also, you are able to see things at that deeper level. So, I will be giving you the main structure of the book, but you are to add the finer details. There may be some topics that will require a bit of research, but this will be obvious to you.

**Me:** So, when I type it up, how do I present it? You are talking to me now in the first person. Is this how it is to be set out, with differentiation made between our voices?

**Jazz:** No, it will not work that way and it will hinder the flow of the book. It needs to be presented as seamless information; that way it will be easier to read. At the end of the day, it is not important whose voice is represented. If a true partnership is to be forged between man and horse, there can be no separation. Our consciousness should merge as one and the book should reflect this unity. Only the content matters, so it will read as if you have written it yourself.

**Me:** Since when did you become so wise and spiritual? I hardly recognise you.

**Jazz:** As you listen to me through your higher self, then I am talking to you from that same higher, soul level; the part of me that is divine and all-knowing. But yes, I have had many incarnations on Earth, so I do carry a great deal of spiritual wisdom. But I don't need to tell you that – you could see it in my eyes the moment I arrived. It was the magnet that drew me to you in the first place.

**Me:** Well, what can I say? Other than we have a book to write, and so had better get moving. I am still in shock by the whole thing, but this session has been truly remarkable and has proven to me beyond a doubt that it is for real. My pen hasn't left the page, neither has it paused. For the first time, I actually believe we can do it. I wonder if this will be the first book co-written by a horse and her human Guardian. Magical barely describes it. Let's begin!

From 12/11/16 until the end of March 2017, I sat with my horse about twice a week, letting the words of the horse flow through. No work was carried out from mid-December until the end of January, as it was too cold, and I was busy. Each session lasted around 30 to 40 minutes, and in everyone, the writing just flowed. There was no pause. No writers block. I can't think of a more effortless way to write than this. One chapter, *"The Abused Horse"*, came about through a dream. For some of the chapters, Jazz would just direct me what I was to write about. So, for example, in Chapter 6 *"The Teaching Horse",* I was told that as I understood the lessons that each of my horses had taught me, then this is what I needed to cover.

By the end of March, there appeared to be sufficient material, so I took my manuscript home to type it up. I have kept the order of the chapters the same as how they came through. When I stop and think about it, I really can't believe how miraculous this process has been. It has been so very different from the first book I wrote, where I carefully thought and planned it.

From my perspective, I really feel like the material was channelled through me by my horse. I would enter the stable with no forethought about what to write. From the moment I put my pen on the paper, I could hear a voice in my head that I was just following. It was an effortless process. I didn't even read it back until I took the manuscript home, and when I read it, I had absolutely no idea what to expect. Would it just be gibberish, with no form whatsoever? Would it even make sense?

With great trepidation, I read the pages. To say I was blown away was an understatement. Not only did it make perfect sense, but it all flowed on beautifully. For the first time, I could see the form the book would take. I feel truly blessed to have been the means through which the horse could express himself. For me, there is no greater honour!

# CHAPTER 3 – THE AWAKENING

*The secrets of the Universe can only be revealed*
*When we are open to receiving them.*
*For when the mind is closed,*
*It is akin to a "no entry sign"*
*Stopping magic and miracles in their tracks.*

My awakening happened in March 2012, after I lost my horse, Tiffany. We had been together for 26 years, and we had shared a very close bond. I do sometimes question *"Why me?"* We all suffer the heartbreak of losing loved ones, so why do other people not witness the same miracles that I did?

I think the answer may be twofold. In the months leading up to losing my horse, I had discovered animal communication. I was reading every book going on the subject. These books were really opening up my mind and heart. Some were so beautiful, that I felt myself connecting to something beyond myself; an invisible force; a love vibration. Call it what you will, but I found my very essence changing and altering. I believe that being in this higher state of vibration opened my heart and mind sufficiently to witness the unfolding miracles.

I also think that my soul purpose is to help connect people to the true essence of the horse. The miracles that were gifted to me were the incentive to get me started on my mission. Without them, I would never have ventured down the spiritual path and this book would never have been born. I recorded the events of my awakening immediately after they occurred, in order to preserve the authenticity. This is my story: -

*The night before I lost Tiffany, I had a beautiful dream; the like of which I have not had before or since. On awakening, I tried desperately to hold onto it, but the details evaded me. My only memory was spending the night with my horse, but not in the physical sense. More on a soul level, where we were completely united and knew each other inside out. The dream affected me so much, that I mentioned it to my husband, who is by no means spiritual. His reaction was typical: I was just mad! Thinking about it now, I always knew that Tiffany and I had an incredible connection. I think it was her way of saying goodbye. But she was also telling me that nothing could ever separate us; that our souls would always be together.*

*Still in a daze from the dream, I went downstairs to make breakfast and turned the computer on. I discovered the next beautiful thing to happen that morning. An animal communication (my first) had been carried out on Tiffany and was sitting in my inbox. It was meant to have been completed a few weeks earlier, but through some strange twist, it had disappeared off the communicators list, so had been delayed until now. Today was clearly the day I was supposed to receive it, and with the events that were to follow, it was destined to become a parting gift. I was blown away – it was a wonderful testimony to our bond and adventures over the years, and it was completely accurate.*

*Before I even ventured up the yard that morning, everything seemed surreal. I had no idea that in just a few short hours, I would lose my soul mate with whom I had spent 26 years. Although it was heart breaking to say goodbye to my wonderful horse, I did draw comfort from the fact that I was with her throughout. Tiffany knew what was happening – she gave a loud neigh to her horse friend in the next field and then to me. She made it very clear that she wanted me to stay with her. While we were waiting for the vet to arrive, she would rest her head on my shoulder, interspersed with walking around in very small circles. When doing this, she would be whinnying the whole time. It struck me as strange at the time – this was not a distressed "Please save me" whinny, but very much a greeting sound. I remembered just before my Nan died, she talked of a little boy and girl at the bottom of her bed whom no-one else could see. Was this the same thing? Had her mother come for her? There was no doubt in my mind that I was saying goodbye. As the vet walked up the path towards us, Tiffany spiralled in circles all the way up the field and collapsed in the gateway. The vet reckoned it was neurological.*

*The rest of the day passed in a haze of misery, as I went home and gave vent to my grief. In-between the tears, I prayed fervently that my horse would be happy, and if possible that I could be given a sign to this effect. I just needed to know that she was happy and safe.*

*How quickly my prayer was answered! The very next day, I was riding along a bridle path with my daughter and her friend, when we spotted a sunflower along the sandy path. I commented that I had never seen a sunflower on a bridleway before, and not one like this – it had a large head, but the stalk was short for a sunflower, being only about 18 inches off the ground. Even more remarkable, it was absolutely perfect. The petals were evenly spaced, and it was without mark or flaw. The next day we rode past it again, but from the other direction. It looked even more surreal, this stunning sunflower next to the sandy path. It is the only time that I regretted having a £7 phone with no camera mode. The thought entered my head that it must be artificial, but as we rode past, there was no mistaking the leaves around its base and the thick stem entering the ground.*

*An hour later, when we rode back, the sunflower had gone. As my daughter expressed her astonishment, my numb, dazed brain clicked into gear and the full significance of what we had seen hit me. This was 9$^{th}$ March, not late summer, when you would expect to see a sunflower, and temperatures had plummeted to -5 degrees centigrade the previous week. Furthermore, this bridleway is used by walkers and riders at the weekend, and yet the only ones to have witnessed it were myself, my daughter and her friend. There was no doubt in my mind that this was the sign I had been so desperate to receive. And what a sign! For me, the sunflower radiates joy and happiness. Nothing could be better proof that my horse was residing in a beautiful place. I also felt instinctively that she wanted me to experience the same joy and happiness. It wasn't just a symbol for her state of happiness, but also what she wanted for me.*

*Although I felt truly blessed and overjoyed to have received such a wondrous sign, and comforted to know my horse was happy, it was still hard to let go of the heartache inside. The thought of not seeing her on a daily basis was hard to bear. On Tuesday morning, I sat crying over my breakfast, wondering how I was going to face heading up the stables that morning. I was to put my friend's horses out, and their stables were right next to Tiffany's. How could I bear to hear them neigh to me, and for Tiff's neigh to be absent? On walking into the yard, my heart was very heavy. I was dreading the usual greeting. Instead, I could not believe what I was hearing, or rather not hearing. Just silence! I can honestly say that it is the only time in 8 years that they have not neighed to me, and the only time that I didn't want them to neigh.*

*Amazed, I stumbled into Esther's stable to change her rug. The horse next to her, a beautiful thoroughbred named Monty, put his head over the wall. Normally, he is very aloof, and if I go to stroke him, he retreats. Today was different. He started nuzzling, kissing and licking me on the side of the neck. Loving this, I told him as much, and the more I praised him, the more intense it became. At one point, he put his head in front of mine and I had to look twice at what I was witnessing. His one eye had filled with water and, very slowly, a trickle ran down his face. To me, there was no doubt that this empathetic horse was picking up on my heartache. Not only this, but he was responding to it, and trying to comfort me. I recalled that he had lost his field mate only six months before – he understood the heartache of loss.*

*As I stood, mesmerised by what I was witnessing, Monty resumed kissing and licking the side of my neck. Up until now, Esther had been quietly standing by, but she suddenly became very interested in what Monty was doing. She looked at him quizzically, with a "What on Earth are you doing?" look on her face, and then unbelievably, she started to mimic what he was doing on the other side of my neck. The next ten minutes passed in a blur. As these two horses gently caressed me, it felt like we were unified in a bubble of harmony and love. Words can't do justice to the sense of empathy and understanding that the three of us were locked into. In all my years of being around horses, I have never had one horse, let alone two, lick my neck so lovingly. And these weren't even my horses. It was only when someone walked into the yard, and shouted "Hello", that the spell was broken, and we all jumped apart.*

*Looking back, I realise something miraculous happened in that stable. The horses didn't just comfort me, they healed me and mended my heart in such a profound way, that even today, a few years on, I can't even comprehend it. I had walked into that stable with my heart breaking, and I walked out with a heart full of joy. I felt incredible happiness, like I had been touched by the Divine. And through those horses, I believe that I had. My perception of my horse's death had changed completely, and I couldn't believe how much I had to be thankful for. It is very hard to explain because it is something that I don't really understand, but from that moment, I completely came to terms with my horse's death and felt only joy instead of heartache. Joy, because I had spent 26 years with the most wonderful horse imaginable, and even at the end, she had been able to transition with very little suffering. Few people experience this sort of blessing.*

*Needless to say, these events have changed my life. I have really opened up to the spiritual aspect of life and my perception of life (and death) has changed completely. From these experiences, I believe that death is only the body dying. I believe that the soul lives on, and our loved ones are always close to us, even though we can't see them. Separation is just an illusion! I also believe that by opening our hearts and minds we can allow those souls to communicate with us, be it through dreams, meditation or other means. And I strongly believe that they want the same peace and happiness for us, as they themselves are experiencing. This is the message I get through all my communications. All they want is for us to experience joy, love and peace.*

*I realise that I was incredibly blessed to have had so much support at such a difficult time, but I do believe that this is available to each and every one of us, if we allow it. I am no more special than the next person. All I did was open my heart and mind and allow the impossible to happen. When we are prepared to take a leap of faith, and suppress our logical mind, the magic really does start to happen!*

So, that is my story and I promise you this; every single word is true. It may sound incredibly far-fetched, and some people may choose not to believe it, but it is exactly what happened. It marked a turning point in my life as I set off down the new path that had opened up to me. In the process, I learned animal communication, became a Reiki master and spent any free time reading or immersing myself in spiritual matters. I experienced many more wonderful happenings, which have been documented in my first book, *"Seeker of the Light."*

It may even be that through the dream Tiffany managed to pass some of her soul onto me. All I know is that, while I was unified with the horses in the healing session, the desire to help them started to rise up within me. At that moment, I felt they were massively misunderstood, and we were missing the bigger picture. I made a promise then and there – I would devote the rest of my life to helping these beautiful souls be better understood. My mission was born!

# CHAPTER 4 – JAZZ'S STORY

*God gave humans intellect and a sophisticated brain.*
*To the horse he gave:*
*Dignity, beauty, humility,*
*Power, strength, majesty,*
*And the desire to harness himself*
*To the whims of mans' dreams.*

Jazz was keen to tell me her life story. As with the other chapters, the words just flowed through me. I found it moving to write, but even more so when reading it back. Seeing things from the horse's perspective is so valuable, as it really teaches us about making empathic connections. This is Jazz's story in her own words.

**Life on a Stud**

I made my appearance on a cold April day, or so I am told. It is hard to recollect much of those early days, but I do remember having a great mum, who was an expert in rearing foals. She was based on a stud farm in Ireland, and I was not her first foal. I think there had been a few before me. By the time I came along, caring for a foal was second nature.

There is no love like a mother's. My memories of those early days are all good – the wonderful sensation of warm milk slipping down my throat and into my belly; the soft caresses and nickers from my mum; and the comfort of her tongue licking me along my neck, especially when I was scared or anxious. Around my mum, I felt invincible. She was always there to protect me. No need to fear danger with my mum around.

It was a fairly large stud, and there was a fair few other foals around. I was never short of playmates. That first summer was just great - such happy, happy days. It was a time for exploring and testing out the world we had been born into. Days of racing around the field and discovering who was the bravest. That was me, by the way. I loved exploring and checking things out; generally putting my nose where it wasn't wanted.

Like they say, all good things come to an end. And so, it was. There was no staying a baby forever! I was weaned at seven months, and for me it was too early. I didn't feel anywhere near mature enough to leave my mum. I still recall the pain of the separation. I really thought my heart would break, and I was so, so scared. How would I stand on my own four feet without my mum to guide and support me? Those first few weeks without her were difficult and scary. I felt I had been wrenched out of paradise, and placed into a situation that was way too overwhelming for a little foal like me. I just wanted it to go back to how it was. In my opinion, foals are taken away from their mum far too early. It should be more of a gradual thing, over a longer period of time. Particularly, for a sensitive foal like I was. It was soul shattering.

I think a part of me has never really recovered from that forced separation. Even though I was placed a long way away from mum, I could still hear her calling for me. It broke my heart that I wasn't able to run to her and feel her comforting muzzle and tongue on my neck. For the first time in my life, I had to face the fact that life wasn't always sweetness and light. I felt lost and alone, and the world suddenly seemed a lot darker. *"Oh mum, please forgive me for not running to you. I would if I could."*

Eventually, I started to adjust to life without mum. I think it took longer for me than it did for the other foals, but in time, my carefree nature started to return. I spent the next few years in a large field with some of the other youngsters, some a couple of years older than me. Once again, we returned to racing each other and kicking our heels up. There were a couple of older mares in the field with us, and they taught us the importance of manners and politeness. There was a fine balance between learning to find your independence and overstepping the mark. These older mares knew when we crossed the line, and they would quietly and quickly put us back into place with a gentle nip on the bottom. Being with these horses really taught me the socialisation skills that would serve me throughout my life. I was well and truly integrated into the rules of horses and understood the pecking order in a herd.

I knew very early on that I wasn't really the horse they had hoped for. With my mother's good breeding, combined with the excellent bloodlines on my dad's side, it was hoped that the union would produce something pretty spectacular. I felt sad to disappoint them. It was made clear to me that my dad had been an amazing and stunning racehorse. In his lifetime, he had taken winnings in the region of £200,000 and he held the record time for completing the Italian Derby, a record that survived for fifteen years.

From early on, it was evident that I hadn't inherited my dad's great turn of speed. It is very disheartening to know that you don't match up; that you aren't good enough. It really knocks the stuffing out of you. Even today, I feel my sensitivities flaring if I am being judged. I am what I am.

Nobody should have to apologise for that. We should all be accepted for who we are.

My future was uncertain. I was going to have to fulfil another role and not the role that was intended for me. It was clear I was never going to be a racehorse or eventer like on my mum's side of the family. What was going to become of me?

**My Polo Playing Years**

A polo yard in Gloucestershire came to my rescue…if you can call it that. They expressed an interest in me and offered to take me on. I was an unusual colouring, being a very dark grey, with hints of dapples and blue roan in my coat; a result of having a silver-grey dam and a sire who was bright bay. I think it was my colouring that first attracted their attention, as well as my good bloodlines. A new life was beckoning. At three years old, it was time to leave my friends and the only home I knew. A new chapter was about to begin.

As you know, I am a highly sensitive horse. To be thrown into the hustle and bustle of such a competitive place was incredibly stressful for me. I was not suited to that type of place. They broke me in not long after I arrived. Some would say I was lucky to have been backed by a highly experienced person. So, call me ungrateful, but I would have preferred a loving and familiar hand on my bridle. It took me a long time to settle into that place and I never felt like I totally belonged. I was like a duck out of water.

Polo work was very forceful. I had a harsh bit put in my mouth and the work was geared towards making me very supple. Once I was broken, a lot of my work was in canter. The training was based on exercises which would enable me to move very easily from side to side, and to be able to stop and go with ease. But that ease never really happened. I just found the work very hard. Although I look athletic, my body just wouldn't go where it was supposed to; or with the speed that was being expected of me. I began to dread the sessions, but any form of protest was met with a severe scolding. Free will was an impossible dream. I felt imprisoned.

The arenas were full of men with over-inflated egos, resulting in demonstrations of high and aggressive energy. They lived for the competitions, with a prevailing attitude of "to win at all costs." I felt overpowered by the noise, adrenaline and high energy, the effect on me being that I became quite withdrawn. A lot of the time I just felt scared, and to cope with being left in the stables for long periods, I learned a coping mechanism. Something that was comforting, filling my body with endorphins. I started weaving. Everything seemed better when I weaved from side to side - an outward expression of my mental torture.

I spent about 2 ½ years on that yard and I am convinced that the only reason for my extended stay was an accident to my leg. I was kicked by another horse and suffered some degree of lameness for a while. By this time, it was very evident that my temperament and lack of suppleness just wasn't suited to a polo yard. But now with an injury, they would have to wait until I was completely recovered if they were to sell me on. So, for a time, I was put out in a field with other injured horses, enjoying their companionship. That was definitely the best time for me while I was there. I could finally just chill out, relaxing for the first time since I had arrived. Once fully recovered, I was put back into work, but this time it was to prepare me for my sale.

There is one good thing to say about the polo yard. Most of the stable hands were lovely – not ego driven like the riders. For the first time in my life, I understood how it was possible to bond with a human. I soaked up the kindness and consideration I was shown. The girls who were in charge of me all understood and related to my sensitive nature, absorbing any pain or unhappiness that I felt. They were so empathetic! I realised that humans do have a soft and loving side. In that respect, they aren't so different from us horses. It was possible to love some humans after all.

Quite a few people came to see me, but Laura was the one I fell for and hoped would buy me. She had such gentle energy; very similar to the girls who looked after me. The day she tried me out, I focused as hard as possible to carry her to the very best of my ability. I needed to win her trust and confidence in me. My efforts paid off! When they told me she was going to be my new owner, I was so made up. It was the very best outcome. Unlike the trepidation I felt before coming to the polo yard, I felt rising excitement at my impending departure. Once again, a new chapter of my life was about to begin. But this time I was filled with hope and optimism. What had I done to be so lucky?

**Life with Laura**

The day of my departure, as they loaded me onto the box, which was to take me to my new home, I did feel an element of sadness; saying goodbye to friends (both human and horse) is never easy. But I also felt excited. There was a great sense of anticipation. My new life was awaiting me, and the grass looked greener.

The next three years spent with Laura were happy years. In my time with her, I changed shape – filling out (an indication of contentment) and my coat became lighter. I was very dark to start with, but after three years I was a lovely dapple-grey colour. And boy, was I chilled! Being with Laura was a stark contrast to the high energy, competitive environment I had escaped from. Not only that, but I had a lot more freedom and a lot more opportunity to just kick my heels up in the field. It was a good life. And Laura was everything I hoped she would be and more. We connected very easily and quickly. She loved spending time with me, particularly grooming and making me look pretty.

As far as work went, Laura worked hard on my trot. At the polo yard, I had worked mainly in canter, so working in trot felt very strange to start with. Initially I found it hard to attain and maintain the rhythm, but eventually it did start to come. The riding was a bit haphazard. Some weeks I was ridden two or three times, then maybe not for a month. But it was fine. I don't have the strongest of backs, so this routine worked for me.

When I first went to Laura, I found myself on a yard from where they used to run regular shows throughout the summer. Laura enjoyed these shows, and I became a regular competitor in showing classes, introductory dressage and show jumping. My jumping was a bit crazy. I had no fear and would jump everything, but my tendency to speed up and flatten over the jumps would have Laura hanging on for dear life. I did go to Cricklands twice and am proud to say that, in my class, no horse was faster. I don't think the people who had to put up all the jumps I knocked down were so impressed though. Oh well, I put speed over accuracy every time!

During my years with Laura, I was as happy as a horse can be. I sensed I wasn't Laura's ideal horse, but in spite of that, she still loved me and didn't hold it against me. She was a good rider and she worked hard at getting me better schooled. My high headedness frustrated her; it was hard to break the habits of the polo training. For the most part, I was pretty laid back. It was hard not to be, coming into such a relaxed environment, a direct contrast to the high energy of the polo yard. Occasionally, I would exhibit crazy thoroughbred tendencies, and I think it was these adrenaline fuelled moments which negatively impacted on Laura's confidence.

One day, whilst jumping, I put in a huge, awkward jump, unseating Laura in the process. She was unhurt, but thereafter I noticed a change in her confidence. Always the calm, confident rider, she started to get tense on occasion. Her energy no longer felt the same. I started to be affected by it, gradually losing my confidence. Things just didn't feel the same. We had lost that connection. Laura never lost her love for me, but she did come to that tough realisation that we weren't right for each other. Once again, I was to be sold on.

**The Schooling Yard**

To prepare me for sale, I was to spend a few months in a big schooling yard. And this was Laura's one bad decision; the only bad decision she made in the time I was with her.

To be fair, she only had my best interests at heart. She thought they would really be able to progress my schooling, increase my suppleness and athleticism. Also, that they would be able to progress my jumping by improving my technique. I needed to develop better rhythm and the ability to see a stride, as well as learning to slow down.

The yard was very big and well-known in the area. At the time of sending me there, there was a lot of preparation going on for the Olympics. They were providing horses for the show jumping section of the pentathlon. Part of the preparation for this was to get the horses used to brightly coloured arenas, so the large ménage was bedecked with brightly coloured poles, fillers, balloons and flowers.

Laura felt she was doing the right thing by me. In her opinion, I was going to a fantastic place, with the expertise available to bring out the best in me. She believed that if I could be produced to my full potential, I would be more in demand – increasing my chances of finding the best possible home. She was not doing this to make more money on me; the cost of sending me to this place would negate any extra profits on the sale. She really believed it was in my best interest and that a brighter future depended on it.

Unfortunately, this is a mistake a lot of owners make. They have no faith in their own ability, feeling that the horse will benefit far more by being sent to the experts. But what they don't realise is this; the bond, connection and trust the horse has with its owner counts for more than the technical expertise out there. We would much rather work with someone whom we are bonded with than with someone who is ambivalent towards us, and who has a deadline to meet. A kind, loving and understanding hand is far more valuable to our training than someone who is under pressure for us to perform.

I accept this arrangement works out fine for some horses, but for those of us more sensitive horses, it can be a disaster. I would really urge people to think carefully before sending their horse away to be brought on. Many a good horse has been ruined by this practice. Trust in your own ability. If you have that bond and connection with your horse, it should be straightforward and will happen naturally.

Well, as you have probably guessed by now, that place was a disaster for me. For all outside appearances, it just didn't have a loving heart in it at all. I was stabled the whole time, which brought all my insecurities to the surface. Once again, weaving became a particularly good habit, relieving my boredom and easing my frustration. The fears that I had managed to bury once again rose to the surface. I felt like a volcano threatening to erupt…it would only be a matter of time!

I found the work very hard. I was ridden most days and if not ridden, I was put on the horse walker. I was just one more horse to exercise and feed.

They had a deadline to meet, which put the pressure on. Would they be able to satisfy the client? Would I be supple and well-schooled enough by the end of my time there? The answer for them had to be yes. Otherwise, the client would be demanding her money back.

They despaired at my high head carriage. In order to rectify this, my head was strapped down. In trot and canter, with my natural crookedness, I found it really hard to balance myself and find the rhythm they were looking for. As you are aware, my back isn't the strongest, so it was painful and uncomfortable to be ridden this way. The jumping didn't really materialise – they recognised my rhythm and balance weren't good enough, although I did do a fair bit of pole and grid work.

Depression started to take hold of me. I felt suffocated and lonely, missing my friends and Laura. *"Please take me home,"* became my mantra. As well as missing the loving energy of home, I missed the freedom and security. Where had I gone wrong to end up here? I just didn't understand it.

The day the volcano finally erupted happened to be the day that Laura came to watch me, anxious to see how I was progressing. My rider felt tenser than usual, not surprising really, as he was under pressure to perform; he needed to demonstrate that they were doing their job and I had improved. Right from the start I could feel his tension. Intuitively, I felt this wasn't going to end well – for him rather than me. I have always been able to read people's energy very easily and I do get affected by it. So, when I feel someone astride me and I pick up their mounting anger and frustration, I start to feel the same emotions building up within me. In this way I am like a mirror – reflecting back the same feelings.

I sensed the man's frustration starting to build, lighting my own fears and insecurities. My brain started to feel scrambled, and I felt incapable of responding to the simplest of commands. Suddenly, it all became too much. I just stopped. He reacted the only way he knew how – stoking the volcano that was about to erupt. As I felt the sharp sting of the whip connect to my side, and the growl of his menacing voice ordering me to *"Walk on,"* the adrenaline coursed through my body faster than a jet plane in full flight. I responded the only way I knew how.

He had no chance of sitting through a full explosion, and I refused to give him that chance. Laura picked up my reins, absolutely horrified by what she had witnessed. Leaving the man to pick himself up, she quietly led me away. The tears coursing down her face, she explained she was going to fetch her box and would be back to pick me up. Thank God I was going home. One of the worst chapters of my life was over.

On arriving home, Laura could see I wasn't myself. Feeling guilty for what she had put me through, she promised me downtime. I was to be turned out in the field for a couple of weeks with nothing to be asked of me. Time to chill and just be a horse again!

Not long afterwards, you came along to view me. You explained you were looking for a long-term project. You had a friend who was a friend of Laura, and she had alerted you to my sale.

Horses, as you know, are experts at reading people. They can quickly pick up on their intent, energy and personality. Some horses are more adept at this than others. I class myself as being pretty proficient in this ability and, as soon as you came into my space, I liked your energy. It felt similar to Laura's – laidback and easy-going. I could sense your loving heart.

When it came to the riding, I wasn't so impressed. Laura had put me in quite a severe bit, and although she knew how to ride me in it – very sensitively and appropriately- you didn't find it so easy. I gave you the benefit of the doubt though. Your reaction to my forwardness was understandable, as you didn't know me. Riding through the hands and not the seat was just not ideal, causing me to keep throwing my head in the air to avoid the pressure.

Nevertheless, we did finish on a good note. You started to adjust – focusing on riding me off your seat and using your mind to instruct me in pace and direction. By the end, we were starting to flow. I was delighted when you expressed an interest in coming back and trying me out on a ride. After all, I could train you to be a better rider. You would soon learn.

**A Forever Home**

Just a few weeks later, I was happily ensconced in my new home. Fate had brought us together and I felt a connection with you from the very first day. I felt your excitement at me coming into your life, as I sensed your calming energy and your love. I picked up on your happiness, reflecting it back at you. Your intentions were good, with no expectations or deadlines to meet. You promised me that it was a forever home and your love was unconditional. Yes, you would like to progress my schooling – not for competition purposes; but just so that by becoming looser and more supple, my body would function better, giving me a better chance of a longer and healthier life. Gradually, I started to relax. And breathe. My future was secure – a privilege afforded to very few horses.

We just rode out together to start with. This was perfect for me, helping me to chill and relax. Being naturally curious, I do enjoy riding in new places, having somewhere new to explore. Having spent so much time riding in arenas, I really enjoyed seeing the sights. I needed this downtime. I loved the slow pace you brought me back into schoolwork and the fact you recognised that it would take as long as it would take. The journey was the important thing, not the destination.

From the very first, you felt instinctively that physically I was compromised in some way. But no amount of body, back or cranial work could really get to the bottom of it. However, progress, although slow, did start to happen. You dispensed with traditional methods, feeling we were just going backwards. You started experimenting with less well known, more holistic methods. In doing so, you learned that not all are as they claim to be. Even though promoting themselves as a true partnering of the horse, you objected to the domination over the horse. As holistic as they appeared, they were still disguising that age old attitude: *"Do as I ask, because I am the boss."*

You were looking for a true partnership, where I could fully express myself and also have choices. You learned to trust your own intuition and instincts. In so doing, you have brought us to a good place. Our progress in the last year has been greater than the rest of the time put together. You found a good instructor, an expert on rider body mechanics and true partnering of the horse. By correcting your crookedness and improving your straightness, this has helped with my issues.

I am now much calmer and relaxed, particularly with the canter work. For such a long time, canter work in the school just triggered those long held, traumatic memories buried deep in my psyche, where I could hear the shouting and feel the adrenaline of horses careering around a polo arena. Tension would invade my body, and my body would respond accordingly, with a high head and hollow back. But now, the story is changing. You are delighting in my canter work – *"Heavenly"* was how you described this week's canters. Thank God for your patience.

So here we are, in this present moment. We both understand that our coming together was no accident. Naturally spiritual, as all horses are, your spiritual journey has also accelerated mine. As you recognised the healer in you, then so I recognised it in myself. It is wonderful that you have given me a voice, allowing me to tell my story. Hopefully, people will find it in their hearts to read this, allowing them to see horses in a different light. As you have come to realise, you can't always take things at face value. There is always something more going on at a much deeper level. So it is with horses. Deep in your hearts and souls, you are already aware of this. You have always known there is more to us than meets the eye. I hope through reading this book, people will open their minds enough to conceive this as a possibility. In a soulful partnership together, horse and man could achieve so much. With man's intelligence, coupled with the horse's power, humility, nobleness and beautiful spirit, you have a match made in heaven.

# PART 2 – THE MULTI-FACETED HORSE

## Chapter 5 – The Spiritual Horse

*Perception is a life changer.*
*Some see horses as dangerous at both ends*
*And uncomfortable in the middle.*
*Others see them as an expensive field ornament*
*Or a means to support the human Ego.*
*Most just see four legs and a tail.*
*I see a spiritual teacher who can take me on a journey of*
*expanded awareness.*

From when I was a very young girl, I seemed to know instinctively that horses had an awful lot of lessons to teach us. Ok, so some of them are pretty obvious. Others, I have only really become aware of more recently. But one thing is for sure – horses are remarkable teachers. It does beg the question, *"Who is training who?"* If I am honest, I would say that I have learned far more from my horses than they have from me.

Since walking my spiritual path, I have carried out a lot of work on myself – trying to find my true self; the part of me that reflects my divine essence. The qualities that I have been aspiring to, I have come to realise, are already firmly entrenched in the nature of horses. I had never really thought about this before, or even been consciously aware of it, but now I recognise that horses are naturally much more tuned into their spirituality than humans. We have become so obsessed with material possessions and what is out there, that we have lost sight of who we truly are. But horses have never forgotten. Recognising this, it is easy to see how the horse can reconnect us to our spiritual self. We only have to look and learn from these ideal role models. I set out below the many lessons the horse can teach us.

**Self- Acceptance**

Unlike us, horses are totally accepting of themselves and are comfortable in their own skin. They don't worry about their physical appearance or concern themselves with how they come across to the other horses. They are always aligned with their true and authentic self and in every moment, they accept that they are enough. They don't need to change themselves and they don't need to change others.

If only we could do the same, we would be far happier. For when you learn to love yourself, you learn to love others too and this makes relationships so much easier. Like the horses, we should stop comparing ourselves to others and stop trying to be a copy of someone else. We are all unique – with our own gifts and talents- all which help bring balance to the world.

Because the horse accepts himself for who he is, judgement of others just does not happen in his world.

**Non-judgemental**

This applies to all animals, and I think it is one of the main reasons why we are so attracted to them. Their ability to be non-judgemental is something we could do with adopting. We make our lives so much harder by judging others. And even when you are aware you are being judgemental, it is so entrenched in human thinking that it is really hard to do something about it.

But animals never judge. For us humans, this is a beautiful revelation and wonderful comfort. To be accepted as you are is something that we really appreciate and treasure, and it is why so many of us find that being around animals is so liberating and comforting.

As a young girl, I was extremely sensitive to people's judgements. I think this was one of the main reasons why I loved animals so much. I felt animals had more sense. They were totally unimpressed by how you looked or how you sounded. For them, it was all about your loving heart. This is probably why a lot of people love animals more than people. Their ability to love us unconditionally, without judgement, makes them very attractive to be around.

**Forgiveness**

This very much ties in with the fact they do not judge. As with people, some horses never get on with each other, but when you watch bonded horses in a field together, you will notice that if one horse acts aggressively towards another, maybe biting or kicking him, the victim never holds it against the perpetrator. In minutes, the row is forgotten, and you will see them happily grazing side by side together. Unlike humans, they do not become bitter and carry that baggage around with them. They instantly let it go. Mentally, this is far healthier for them.

It isn't just other horses that they forgive. The same attitude is adopted with people. Time and time again, I have seen people treat horses badly – being verbally and physically abusive. But on another day, when that person has a different attitude about them and greets their horse affably, that same horse will greet them with a loving whinny. In these situations, I am always awestruck by the ability of the horse to forgive.

I believe that it is this quality in the horse that has helped them serve us so nobly and selflessly all these years. At times, we have treated the horse abominably and still continue to do so. We have eaten them, used them to carry us in war, but we have also systematically killed them, just for being in our space, or because they have outlived their useful life.

Still today, in parts of the world, they are treated barbarically. Yet, despite all this, the horse still turns up for us, and tries his hardest to serve us in the best way he can. He refuses to give up on us. This lesson in forgiveness is a very important one for us humans. By holding onto our grievances, it causes us untold damage. Hatred eats away the soul of the hater, not the hated. In short, it does not serve us. Like the horse, we need to learn to let go.

**Ability to Always be Truthful**

Whatever anyone thinks, horses never lie or deceive. They are just not wired to do this.

So many times, I have heard people say that the horse pretended to be lame because he didn't want to do something. But this is just not true. Horses' brains don't work that way. So, for example, if the horse is sound out on a ride, but shows slight lameness in the ménage, it isn't because he is bored riding in an arena and is pulling a "sickie." There is clearly a physical issue that is disguised when you ride out. It may be the deeper going in the ménage is highlighting a problem, or maybe doing circles with your horse is putting more pressure on a sore joint.

Sometimes you have to be a Miss Marple and put your thinking head on, but one thing is for sure: the horse is not lying. You definitely have a problem somewhere. The horses' ability to never lie does enable a lot of information to be accurately downloaded to us.

**Ability to Live in the Present Moment**

Unlike us, horses live very much in the present moment. They don't dwell on the past, and they don't think about the future. Every day offers a new beginning – the potential for a clean slate and a fresh start. The day before has had a line drawn under it. There is only the now – a beautiful place to just be.

Spiritual people understand the importance of this concept. There have been many books written on the subject. The whole idea behind meditation is to learn to be fully present in the current moment, the power of now. Horses can teach us so much about this skill.

Jazz has taught me an awful lot about living in the now. She has encouraged me to let go of all my aims and ambitions, and to just accept what is happening in the present moment. This has been a real revelation for me and has made me a lot happier. It really is the best way to live.

## The Ability to Zone Out

Horses regularly zone out. Their ability to fall into a light sleep at the drop of a hat is akin to a trance or meditative state. This is very therapeutic, and horses are so lucky to have this ability.

Zoning out involves splitting the conscious and unconscious mind. The conscious mind is still present, alert to danger. As prey animals, horses always need this ability to stay present and alert as their life can depend on it, but the unconscious mind can be elsewhere. Very much like the human who meditates, they take themselves somewhere more attractive. Particularly for those horses who lead far from ideal lives, this is a great coping mechanism.

This is something us humans could well take on board. Whenever we start to feel stressed, we should allow ourselves just five minutes to take time out. Closing your eyes and breathing deeply, can help you connect to the calm and all that is. This is something that the horses have full mastery over, and something which we would be well-advised to emulate.


## Power of the Herd

Horses thrive best in the herd, for this is the most natural thing for them. They are very much social animals, and foals who are brought up in a herd quickly learn the herd hierarchy and the social rules that are in play.

Every single horse in the herd has a role to play and a placing in that group. But they are all very much connected to each other, understanding that far more can be achieved by working together, rather than being separate from each other.

Even when horses aren't in a herd but are in separate paddocks, it is still easy to see how connected they are. Sometimes, I will be in the field watching them and will notice five or six heads shoot up in unison. They will all turn round in their alert stance, all gazing in the same direction, their bodies parallel to each other. I am always hypnotised by this – it is like awareness telepathically shoots through the whole herd, uniting them as one single horse, rather than six separate horses.

Man is becoming increasingly separated, not only from other humans, but from nature and from his true authentic self. We need reminding that we are part of a connected whole. The power of the herd can remind us that much more can be achieved when we all work together. Horses have never lost this connection.

**Ability to Read Energy**

Even people who have been around horses all their lives are often not fully aware of how able horses are to read energy. Horses react to people – not by how they look, how they speak, or what they say, but by the energy they carry. Horses don't see the person; they feel the energy. Which is why your horse may be happy to be caught and interact with you one day but want nothing to do with you at another time.

Some horses are more sensitive to energy than others. Generally, the more highly bred horses such as thoroughbreds, whose senses tend to be more heightened anyway, will be more sensitive and reactive to energy than the laidback types. Abused horses are also often more sensitive to energy. These horses have developed an inner compass to the moods of the people around them. As a form of protection, they have had to develop a more heightened awareness of picking up energy. This is why abused horses often make such good therapy horses – they have become so adept at reading energy.

Jazz is incredibly sensitive to energy. This can be a good thing and a not so good thing. It benefits us when we are working together on our groundwork in the school. On a good day, when we are both focused and in tune together, I only have to think about increasing my energy to get an upward transition response. To get a downward one, I concentrate on dropping my energy, and Jazz responds beautifully. On a really good day, I only have to think it and it happens; the same with the riding - I just concentrate on using the energy in my body, rather than using aids to get a response.

But her sensitivity to energy can also have drawbacks, as she sometimes picks up negative energy. There is a field opposite the yard where we are allowed to ride, and at the top end of the field there is a huge open gate which, when you ride through, opens onto a bridle path. Right from the start, Jazz did not like riding through this opening and it took about two years for her to be comfortable with it. If on our own, she would start showing reluctance to go forward about 50 feet from the gate. Eventually, as we neared the gate, she would plant and refuse to move. It wasn't so bad if we were riding with another; she would just insist that we rode behind them. It was very strange, because she had no issues going through any other gates. In the end, I just came to the conclusion that she was picking something up energy wise. Perhaps something really bad happened in that gateway. There are signs that people may have lived there in the past - there are some bricks to the right of the gate, suggesting there was a building there at some point and there are rock houses just around the corner.

Interestingly, someone on the yard told me a story about a yard they were on previously. All the horses refused to go through a gate. It transpired that many years earlier they used to slaughter pigs on that very spot. So maybe something similar had happened at Jazz's bogey gate. Other horses I have ridden have also shown some resistance walking towards this gate, so you never know!

Around horses, we need to be more vigilant of our energies and feelings. A bad day at the office may make an evening ride an attractive proposition. But if you are still carrying bad thoughts and negative or angry energy, it is not such a good idea to interact with a sensitive horse. Often, these are the times when the horse will refuse to meet you half-way. All it does is worsen the bad mood, heightening the feeling that the whole world is against you, including your horse. Having witnessed this so many times, I have lost count of people complaining, *"I have had such a bad day, and now my horse just refuses to co-operate."*

Recently, I was able to prove to myself just how much our energy affects our horses. There is a horse on the yard who is difficult to catch, and his owner always uses a bucket to catch him. On a day when he didn't want to come near me, I sat at the edge of his field and sat down to meditate. If I changed my energy, would this horse react to me differently? I concentrated on connecting to divine source, focussing my thoughts on love, joy and gratitude. I imagined a beautiful white light enveloping and surrounding me. Quite suddenly, my peaceful repose was broken. Feeling a shove in my chest, I opened my eyes to find the horse, who hadn't wanted to come near me ten minutes ago, was now asking for me to catch him, put the headcollar on and interact with him. What a result!

This ability in the horse is a great training tool for our emotional functioning. By finding the inner calm within us, we have a better chance of interacting with our horse more productively.

### Ability to Sense the Lie

To some degree, this does tie in with the above. Horses are masters at sensing the truth behind the smile. They can really see what lies behind the mask, sensing any incongruence a mile away. Again, this is a more pronounced ability in sensitive and abused horses.

This ability has been used to great effect in equine therapy centres. In these spaces, people can turn up with big smiles on their faces, seemingly happy and chatty, but hiding deep emotional or mental trauma. They will find that the horses just do not want to interact with them, or even be in their space. It is only when they break down and the trauma comes to the surface, that the horses will start interacting with them and be happy to be around them. Linda Kohanov explores this in her fascinating book *"Riding Between the Worlds"*. Linda herself has an equine assisted therapy centre, and her book very clearly demonstrates the ability horses have to highlight people's hidden emotions and feelings, forcing them to acknowledge and deal with them.

My first pony, Smokey, was adept at seeing the person behind the mask and reading the energy of people. He had been bought by a male dealer out of a sales ring, and he particularly objected to male energy. I think he found it too aggressive. But he adored my dad. And it is no coincidence that my dad is an extremely gentle and loving man.

Not only did he object to strong, male energy, he was able to detect troublemakers a mile away. On one occasion, I was riding him around my housing estate, when a girl from school walked past. She was not a nice girl and was eventually expelled from school for being violent, but I was amazed at my pony's adverse reaction to her. He literally goggled at her, like she was carrying the devil himself on her back, and shot across the other side of the road, refusing to take his eyes off her.

It never ceases to amaze me the feedback horses give about people. Unlike humans, they are so tuned into their inner senses and intuition, that they literally can see people as they really are.

**Ability to Mirror**

This is something else that I have only learned about in the last few years. Like the ability to read energy and to sense the lie, it is another quality in the horse that has been used to great effect in equine assisted therapy.

Horses do have the ability to mirror the person they are working with. So, for example, say that person is depressed and very closed down, with an inability to move their life forward. The horse can mirror this by refusing to move forward with them. Pass the horse to another person, and the horse will move forward freely again. I have actually witnessed this for myself, so I know it to be true.

Therapists use this ability in the horse to reveal the blocks and traumas in their patient's life. For instance, they will ask their client to walk over some poles on the ground. They may ask the client to think of their childhood. If the horse then stops, it is an indication that there is blocked trauma in the client relating to their childhood. By using this ability, the therapist can then get to the bottom of the problem.

Horses don't just mirror emotional and mental blocks either. They can also mirror physical issues. So, a horse who develops asthma or skin conditions can be mirroring these afflictions in their owner. I have heard of two people in the UK who have opened clinics to help with problems afflicting both the owner and their pet or horse. They reckon about two-thirds of people and animals who pass through their doors are actually mirroring each other's symptoms. This is very interesting, because it highlights how deep the bonds go between animal and owner.

**Lack of Ego**

One of the biggest stumbling blocks for humans, and the thing that separates us from our true, authentic self, is our ego. It is our ego that causes us to be insecure, jealous, competitive, controlling, judgemental, fearful and aggressive. In fact, all our negative qualities stem from the ego's need to take control. The horse, on the other hand, does not have an ego.

I find it interesting that, despite horses having no ego, the horse world is dominated by the human ego in all its worst forms. From the moment we start hanging around horses and start learning how to ride, we have it drummed into us that we are in control of the horse, and we must teach him obedience and respect. In other words, we are running the show, and the horse just needs to obey our commands. If the horse doesn't comply, he is labelled difficult and disrespectful.

I do think attitudes are changing though. I still have books from when I was a child, and it makes me shudder when I thumb through some of them. We were taught that in any disagreement with your horse, you must always have the last say – if you were to give up on something, then you could guarantee that your horse would be twice as problematic next time you asked him to do it. The horse was just never allowed to say no or have any opinion on anything that was detrimental to you, the rider.

Luckily, we have moved away from this way of thinking. People are starting to look more closely at why the horse may be objecting, and there is more emphasis on listening to the horse and deciphering what it is he is trying to tell us. But we still have an awful long way to go, as the horse still has very little say in when, where and how he is ridden, or how he is kept. He is still a slave to our ambitions and timescales.

The whole environment of the horse can be very competitive; indicative of the human ego running the show. Not only in the way we train our horses and relate to them, but also relating to the competitions we enter. Whereas humans are highly competitive, horses care absolutely nothing about winning prizes, or trying to appear better than their horse comrades. They do not care a jot whether they win or lose.

What they do care about is enjoying the things you do together – be it competitions or just hacking out. From a horse's point of view, unless you are enjoying what you do, then what is the point? This attitude is something we could really learn from because I for one believe this wholeheartedly. Now I am older, unlike when I was younger, I have absolutely no interest in winning prizes or rosettes. I have entered a few competitions and I have done it for the love of it, rather than trying to beat other people. Those competitions where Jazz has given her all, and we have flown around the jumps in total enjoyment and harmony, are worth far more to me than the rosettes we have won. Competing as an older rider, with absolutely no interest in the outcome, is far more enriching and enjoyable, than when I used to compete in my teens and twenties, where my nerves used to get the better of me.

This is the thing with the ego: it stops you enjoying and living in the moment. And it can act as a real barrier between the true partnering of horse and rider. Through my own journey, I really believe that horses are trying to lead us away from our ego-centred natures. In so doing, we create a space where we can hear the horse more clearly. It is in this space that the relationship between human and horse can really grow and flourish. This has been a particularly big learning curve for me, and I discuss my personal experience of it in the next chapter.

**Inclination to Joy**

Any horse lover cannot fail to be impressed by the horse in full flight – galloping and kicking his heels up. Horses have a natural inclination towards joy, and most horses, even the older ones, seem to spend some part of the day having a crazy moment.

If you watch foals, they spend their whole day eating, sleeping and having fun. They relish their sense of freedom and being able to gallop around the field, playing with other youngsters. A lot of horses retain this inclination towards joy, even when they are in their 20's and 30's. In fact, my horse Tiffany, still liked to race the horses in the neighbouring field in her 30's. She would get very excited if the ground was covered in snow, galloping and bucking for all she was worth. She would become really playful, like a youngster again. It was wonderful to see.

When this freedom is taken away from horses, they can become withdrawn and depressed. Both Jazz and my daughter's pony, Silver, have had periods where they have had enforced stable rest (due to illness/injury), and both found it very difficult to deal with. Jazz was very stressful, and Silver became depressed. But the joy they expressed when they were returned to the field was wonderful to see. Racing up and down, bucking and rearing, enjoying their freedom to the full, really brought tears to my eyes. They both fully expressed their joy and happiness, leaving me in no doubt whatsoever where they preferred to be.

Being around horses can really connect us to the joy of being. We are reminded of our inner child, and the need to be playful, not taking life too seriously. Like the horses, leave your worries behind and rejoice in the ability to just kick up your heels and have fun. *"Let go"* the horses beseech us.

**Connection to Nature**

Unlike us humans, who have really lost our connection to nature, horses are still very connected to the natural world. They understand the seasons and they like nothing more than being out in the fresh air, kicking their heels up and feeling the warm sun on their back.

Some of their habits are not really fully appreciated by us humans. For instance, we believe that when horses roll, covering themselves with dirt, it is helping to provide an extra layer for warmth, as well as protection from the rain and flies. This is all true, but there is also another reason, as Jazz tells me. It also provides them with a connection to Mother Earth – helping to ground them and bring them "down to Earth." You have also probably seen your horse sniffing the ground and being very selective where he rolls. They are seeking out the soil which has the best energetic properties. Jazz telling me this astonished me. How come I had never heard this before? A couple of years after Jazz had enlightened me with this information, I read in a journal that one of the species of bacteria in the soil, *M Vaccae,* has been found to affect the brain and increase stress resilience. Science is finally catching up!

Just weeks after Jazz telling me this, I witnessed an event which proved it. Jazz was in season, and unusually for her, she had been flirting outrageously with two of the geldings in the neighbouring field. It didn't take long for one of them to rear, bringing the fence down as he landed on it. In the blink of an eye, Jazz was happily ensconced in the field with the two geldings, and it took very little time before she was joined at the hip with one of them.

Attempts to catch either of them were absolutely fruitless. They were having none of it. Very wisely, they recognised that being caught meant separation and the end of their fun. So, hooves up to that idea! As they happily galloped and cavorted around together (looking amazing in the way that flighty horses float above the ground), I decided to retreat and try again a few hours later.

Seeing them quietly grazing side by side, encouraged me to try again about three hours later. The sight of me just resulted in a replay of their earlier antics, so I retreated again. Five minutes later, I noticed Jazz rolling. As she stood up, her companion went down, and he vigorously started rolling too. I decided to put the grounding theory to the test. Would the adrenaline have dissipated? As I approached the horses, I sensed a completely different energy. They were calm, their heads lowered and their eyes soft - and yes - they let us just walk up to them without even the slightest movement of their heads, as their head collars were placed on. Success!

Some years later, Jazz would prove to me again how important that roll in the dirt truly is. Their peace of mind can depend on it!

Jazz had spent ten days in hospital with inflammation around her heart and lungs, and an infection in one of the valves of her heart. She had been very poorly, hence the time in hospital.

Returning home, I was acutely aware of how "fizzy" her energy appeared and how erratic she seemed. Her eyes were darting everywhere, and her ears were barely still. I had been told that it was very important with her heart condition to keep her calm and quiet, yet seeing her in this flighty state, I worried how I was going to achieve it.

As she bounced around the yard after coming off the lorry, it suddenly occurred to me what she needed. A damn good roll!

I led her into the medical paddock. For five or ten minutes she proceeded to walk erratically around the paddock, with me hanging gainly onto her rope. She wasn't just sniffing the ground; she was licking it too. Spot chosen, her legs buckled, and she moaned and groaned ecstatically, as she rolled vigorously and thoroughly in the sandy soil. Her joy and relief were palpable!

As she rose from the ground, shaking herself, I couldn't fail to notice the altered expression in her eyes. They were soft and gentle, and the whole energy of her being was completely altered. Calm and settled, the only thing that now interested her was the grass. She had ten days of catching up to do!

From that moment on, Jazz was the perfect patient. She was only allowed short stints in the paddock for the first couple of days, gradually building up the time, but it mattered not. She came when called, she was calm and willing at all times, and took her medicine (six syringes a day) happily and without fuss.

This should raise important questions and considerations. How about stabled horses who do not have access to a field/paddock to roll in? How about horses who are rugged, and fly sheeted? Yes, they can roll, but they are still missing out on a "mud bath" and those vital nutrients.

Once again, I am humbled by the wisdom of my horse. They have much to teach us! It is up to us to catch up with their innate wisdom and allow them what they need.

In the wild, horses are very tuned into their bodies, knowing exactly which grasses, plants and herbs they need to eat to keep themselves healthy. If they do have a health issue, they know instinctively what they need to eat from nature's medicine cabinet in order to help heal. Unfortunately, due to their domestication, we are now putting them in paddocks where they no longer have the capacity to pick out the foodstuffs they might need. They now have no choice in the matter.

But this instinct is still there, and some herb companies do allow you to purchase a small amount of various different herbs and offer them to your horse, to see which one he picks out for his liking. We tried this out with Jazz and Silver. Jazz picked out the valerian root, which made sense, as it is supposed to help with relieving stress and tension. Silver's choice surprised us though. He is a very food orientated pony, so we expected him to like all of them. But he didn't. He only picked out one and that was the nettles.

A couple of years on, and this choice would make perfect sense. He developed laminitis, triggered by Equine Metabolic Syndrome (EMS). And it turns out that dried nettles help with the circulation in the feet. Also, I have since read an article which proclaimed that dried nettles are a beneficial supplement for horses suffering from EMS. This just proves how adept horses are at knowing what they need for their health. It is such a shame that we limit and restrict them from making the right choices.

There have been times in my life when I have been amazed by the horses' ability to read their environment and also the weather. My first pony, Smokey, was kept in a very natural, herd environment and he was the herd leader. One day, I noticed him gather the horses together in a very tight-knit group, while he proceeded to canter around them. I was fascinated by this, not understanding why he was doing it. About an hour later, a storm struck. Suddenly, the reason for this behaviour became clear. He was trying to protect them and keep them in a safe area – at the bottom of the hill and away from the trees. But I was just amazed that he knew a storm was brewing, because I certainly hadn't sensed it.

On another occasion, I was riding my horse Tiffany through some woods, when she suddenly stopped, refusing to move forward. There was a bit of mud in front of us, but it didn't look any different to any other mud we had walked through. At this point, I had only owned Tiffany for about three months, so I hadn't been with her long enough to know this was highly unusual. In time, I would come to realise that this was a horse who hated standing for anything. Forward movement was the only thing she knew. So, I didn't even think that something might be wrong. I just believed my horse had suddenly become averse to a bit of mud. So, I pushed, and I pushed. Unrelentingly! My poor horse in the end felt she had no choice. Resigning herself to our fate, she proceeded to walk through it.

Everything happened so quickly, but the next thing I knew, I was sitting on the floor, watching my horse battle her way out of a bog. Her efforts to get out had thrown me clear, but it took her a bit more time to free herself from that mud that had encased her about three-quarters of the way up her legs. I just felt horrified, and so sorry for what I had put her through. Luckily, my horse was fine, and I was able to remount before heading home. But I promised her that I would never put her through anything like that again. In future, I would heed what she was telling me because she was clearly a lot wiser than I was.

As is evident from this chapter, horses have an awful lot they can teach us. To further our spiritual development, we could read books and attend courses, but really all we need to do is look at those four-legged friends in our paddocks and observe the way they relate to each other, and the way they deal with life. They can be our spiritual teachers and gurus. In the next chapter, I go on to explore the idea that individual horses also have lessons they can teach us. I believe that there is no randomness to the horses that we pick to be our companions or riding partners. We get the horses we need that can teach us the lessons we need to learn at that specific time in our lives. It is no accident!

# Chapter 6 – The Teaching Horse

*Unity with the horse can never be found in domination. Instead, it is created in stillness, born from an empathic and loving heart.*

For myself, I have only ever bought three horses. When I look back at the lessons these horses taught me, I realise it was no coincidence that each of them came into my life when they did. Each horse was very different in their character and personality, but they all had profound lessons to teach me, and strangely, the lessons they each taught me were the lessons I needed at each of those different stages in my life.

I feel very blessed to have had these wonderful souls in my life, and very grateful for their teachings. I want to devote most of this chapter to outlining my journey with each horse in turn.

**Smokey**

From the moment I first properly encountered a horse at about 4 years old, I was in love. All my dreams henceforth revolved around owning one of these beautiful animals. I don't know where my love of animals originated from, as neither of my parents or grandparents were into animals – they had never even owned a pet. The funny thing was, my sister, who was two years younger, also loved animals. It was something new for our family.

My parents were very firmly opposed to my horse loving tendencies. My dad saw them as expensive, and my mum viewed them as dangerous. They finally conceded to allowing me riding lessons when I was nine. The next few years were blissfully spent exercising horses for people or working in riding stables. I was as horsey obsessed as it was possible to be.

One magical day when I was fourteen, my dad amazed me by announcing that my sister and I could have a pony. He had come to the realisation that it was a craze that was never going to go away. Furthermore, he was getting a bit tired of ferrying us around, as the pony we were exercising was 7 miles away. It had been decided that, as my mum was going back to work, a pony would be affordable. The only condition to having a pony was that my parents would have no part to play in it at all. We would keep him at a neighbouring farm, and it was up to us to get ourselves there and back. Fine by us! The thought of not having parents around to keep an eye on proceedings, leaving us to our own devices, was just perfect.

To say we were delighted was a complete understatement. I had spent nearly every minute of my life dreaming of this moment. Ecstatic doesn't even get close to describing it! I was giving my dad no chance to go back on his word though! That Friday night, I scoured the Express and Star to see if there was anything suitable. In those days, this was the only way you could find local horses for sale, other than word of mouth. I saw the advert for Smokey, 14hh, 8 years old, grey Connemara/Welsh cob- ideal first pony. And that was how he came into our lives.

We bought Smokey off a male dealer, who had bought him out of a sales ring. I think he had spent his life being dominated by men, so for him, being owned by two girls was a real novelty. And boy, did he take advantage. He was turned out with a herd, on what was probably a 60-acre field – it was huge. That was how horses were generally kept in those days, as land was more plentiful than now. It was certainly more beneficial for them. Not so good for the owners though, particularly if you were like us and had a pony that was making the most of his freedom. We spent most of that summer connecting more with the grass and finding four leaf clovers than connecting with our pony.

So, the first big lesson for us with this pony was patience. A lot of time in those early months was spent sitting in the field, just trying to win his trust. And when we did, and he was easier to catch, another problem materialised. He would just refuse to move. Trying to lead him up to the stables just took forever. When it came to being ridden, he would be so lazy – it was hard to get him moving. This seemingly dominant, stubborn pony had learned that he could take advantage of two very easy-going young girls, and he was going to milk it for all he was worth. Who could blame him? Like any parent of young children knows, it is a very similar sort of thing. They know just how far they can push the boundaries and get away with things.

I think the turning point came when my blacksmith told me that I needed to toughen up with him – he would kill me if I carried on letting him get away with things. This was certainly an exaggeration! Although Smokey was herd leader, he had never showed any aggressive tendencies to us or the other horses. But the blacksmith saying this did make me look at myself much closer.

I came to the realisation that I did need to become firmer and to start setting very clear boundaries, as it was obvious that he was taking advantage of our naturally placid personalities. From that moment on, I made it clear we would stand no more nonsense. When he stopped in the field, we would keep tapping him with a crop, stopping only when he started to move. Unconsciously, we were using the pressure and release technique, and it worked like a dream. This could be too intimidating for some horses (and would have been so for my next two horses), but it worked well for him.

The strange thing is that, from the moment we became firmer with him and started setting clear boundaries, there was a huge shift in the relationship between us. He suddenly started to respect us. And with that respect, came love. He was no longer the pony who didn't want to be caught. Instead, as soon as he caught sight of us, he would raise his head in the air, trumpeting his greeting for all to hear, then he would come racing over at full gallop. And he would spend as long as you wanted, licking your hands. At heart, this dominant, bossy pony had a very soft and loving nature. We had just needed to press the right buttons to uncover his true personality.

All this love was saved exclusively for my sister and I; he refused to let anyone else catch him. If anyone else tried to groom him, he would pull faces at them and would turn his bum on them.

This lesson was very valuable. It was clear to us that horses don't just want to be spoiled with food, treats and love. To love back, they actually need to have respect for you. And to have this respect, they do need to see you as someone who can create consistent and fair boundaries. For my sister and I, it was real initiation into the herd thinking mentality.

But this lesson in boundary setting went way beyond horsemanship skills. Being the shy, sensitive and easy-going teenager I was, I needed this lesson that Smokey was giving me. It was important that I learned to take back my power and not let myself be walked all over; a lesson that would be as valuable in dealing with people, as it was in dealing with horses.

The other lessons Smokey taught us were perseverance and courage. In those days, most children would compete in gymkhanas at the local show. In the early days, Smokey would put in little effort, just slowly trotting up and down in the races, meaning we were usually last by a long way. But a few years later, once he had really attained the measure of these races, he would be flying.

Similarly, with his jumping. He had a superb jump. I have actually witnessed him walking up to a five-bar gate and jumping over it. Another time, when I was holding him while shutting a gate, a cow put his head over the fence behind us. Smokey jumped the chest-high fence from a standstill, clearing the barbed wire that ran along the top. In fact, he became a bit of a monkey for popping over the fencing around the field. He loved the fact he could jump out and back in again at will.

He was certainly one of the best pony jumpers I had ever come across, but unfortunately these talents were wasted at the shows. He hated fillers, particularly boards. And shows at the time just loved them. Even in the clear round, every jump tended to consist of the dreaded filler. We learned the lessons of courage and humility – spending about 20 minutes in the clear round. The sight of a filler had Smokey approaching it very slowly and cautiously, eyes bulging out his head. He would creep up to it and sniff it, before finally deciding it was safe to jump. Nevertheless, any subsequent rounds would be clear, because once he had learned they weren't going to jump up and bite him, he was fine with them. Until the next show, when you would go through the whole process again. Seven years of this, and he finally learned to jump them first time. Pretty good perseverance I should say!

The other good lesson Smokey taught us was 'stickability'. He was probably the spookiest pony I had ever come across. He never planted or refused to go past anything, but he would shy violently at things. In the early days, this meant we spent a great deal of time on the floor. This was made worse by the fact that wherever you were, Smokey would gallop home and jump in the field, racing up and down with his tack still on. Eventually, I developed a really good seat, staying with him even when he whipped sharply around in canter.

My sister and I joke even now that it is a miracle we survived our teenage years. Most good rides were only accessible by negotiating busy main roads. When we first had him, the sound of a bus or lorry behind him would have him galloping off up the road. Amazingly, despite regular riding on roads, we all survived intact without a single accident. Clearly someone was looking out for us, and it was not our time to pass. Needless to say, we kept our parents in blissful ignorance.

Smokey had a great sense of humour – he taught us to laugh and not take things too seriously. He had a habit, when entering the clear round jumping, of refusing to move until he had emptied his bowels, irrespective of whether he needed to go or not. There were hilarious moments where he would be chased by kids waving sticks to get him moving – to no effect whatsoever. No amount of pressure would make him budge until he had performed his ritual. He also had the habit of stopping in front of the brush fence and taking some in his mouth, before trotting around the arena, displaying his wares to all the laughing crowds. I guess, for shy kids like me and my sister, this was all really good training. We certainly became accustomed to people looking and laughing at us.

Over time, Smokey trained us to be not only competent riders, but also gave us loads of confidence. Most ponies, in comparison, seemed pretty straightforward and reliable, so we never hesitated in helping and dealing with the problems other people were having with their horses. Around horses I took on an entirely new persona. I was able to leave my shy, retiring self at home, and become this confident, knowledgeable person, who would approach any new people on the yard with offers of help.

I look back at those teenage days spent with Smokey with much nostalgia. We fully exploited the joys of pony owning. Over the years, Smokey transformed from a stubborn and objecting pony, into a loyal and trusting friend with whom we had loads of fun. There were far more places to ride off road in those days, with no restrictions. We would spend hours exploring new places, making it a time of great outdoor adventures. In doing so, an amazing bond was formed with this pony, born from all the fun and enjoyment we were having. They were wonderful years, and I wouldn't have changed them for the world.

Seven years with Smokey, my confidence soaring, I really felt the urge to buy a young horse who I could bring on. By this time, I had outgrown Smokey in terms of size and ability, but I still loved him dearly and knew I could never sell him. He had developed into a really lovely, capable pony, so I knew it would be fairly easy to find a young rider who would take him on. In the resulting years, he taught a few children to ride competently, and eventually one kind girl took him on permanently, until the end of his life at 33.

I disappeared out of his life when he was about 24. I was getting married, and we had bought a house about 40 minutes away. As Smokey had been at that farm since he was 8 years old, I made the tough decision to leave him there with the girl he would spend the rest of his life with. Although I left Smokey in really good hands, and deep in my heart I knew it was the right thing for him, there has always been an element of guilt that it was someone else caring for him in his twilight years and not me. It seemed a betrayal to the amazing bond we shared, and part of me will always shed tears that I wasn't with him in those final years. Horses really do leave their hoofprints in our hearts.

**Tiffany**

At the age of 21, I started looking for a young, unschooled horse. With a limited budget, it was a difficult find. The horses I looked at either seemed to have physical issues or were plainly unsuitable.

Eventually, Tiffany came onto my radar. At 8 years old, she was older than intended, but I was assured she rode like a four-year-old, having been turned away in a field for the last few years. A thirteen-year-old girl had bought her, but three months on, she had completely lost her nerve and wanted nothing more to do with her. She was kept at a riding school/livery yard and was being exercised by a girl who worked there.

From the moment I cast eyes on Tiffany, I knew she was the one. It really was love at first sight. She was a pretty, 15.1hh dark bay thoroughbred cross pony type, with a white star. True to word, she was very green, but I could see past this. I was struck by her honest, genuine nature and the fact she was trying so hard to do the things that were asked of her, even though she was finding it difficult. This was a horse who would really give her heart and soul. I bought her there and then – no second try.

Tiffany proved to be everything I had hoped for and more. She really was an extraordinary horse. From the very first day we were bonded, she was neighing and galloping up to me in the field whenever I appeared. And that bond continued to grow. After Smokey (well, certainly the early years with him), she seemed very straightforward and easy. In many ways, she was the complete opposite. She was extremely brave and bombproof. I could ride her past anything; she never shied or made a fuss. Whereas Smokey was always a pony you needed to push on and be quite bossy with, Tiffany had unbelievable energy, but she never used it against you. Also, she only needed the gentlest of requests. Desperate to please, she proved to be one of the most amazing horses I have encountered. Schooling and bringing on this athletic, forward, and willing horse was an absolute joy.

The biggest lesson from having this wonderful horse in my life was discovering how harmonious and joyful a bond between horse and human can be. Riding, when you have complete trust and confidence in each other; and when you can go anywhere and do anything together, is just so incredibly magical. The timing couldn't have been more perfect. In many ways, my twenties were quite a difficult time. I was in a job I had just fallen into, and the pressures of the job were overwhelming at times. Added to this was the stress of having to take professional exams. At one point, I was working with some very difficult people, all men, who were really trying to undermine me. My confidence was at an all time low. On top of this, I entered a relationship, which proved to be emotionally draining at times. In the midst of all this, my horse was a shining light, keeping me upbeat and positive in these darker times. Every moment spent with her was a joyous escape.

It is very easy to journey through life, not really appreciating what you have, or taking it for granted. But there was not one minute of my time spent with Tiffany that I didn't give thanks for. And I don't doubt for a minute that this intuitive, gentle horse was totally aware of my deep love for her. Because this was another of her amazing talents – she was so intuitive to the point I actually believe she was psychic. And there were times when she seemed to be sharing this gift with me. This is explored more fully in the chapter, *'The Psychic Horse'*.

To have 26 years, riding as well as just hanging out with the same horse, is a blessing that few people experience. After my guilt of not being able to care for Smokey in his final years, I was determined not to make the same mistake again. I wanted to devote all my attention to Tiffany- there would be no buying a younger horse.

It was a decision that was to reap untold rewards. Even in her thirties, Tiffany still had incredible energy. Aged thirty, I moved her to another yard, along with two of her friends. She was so excited by the new, off-road riding that I was consulting feed companies as to how I could calm her down. Some days we would ride out in the morning for 2 ½ hours, with her jogging the whole way, only for her to be racing the horses in the adjoining field in the afternoon. No other horse on the yard could keep up with her fast walk. And she still looked amazing. If it wasn't for the grey in her coat, you could have mistaken her for a young horse. It just wasn't possible to see her as an old horse.

When she was thirty-two, she developed arthritis in her fetlock joint, but joint supplements and painkillers kept her going for another two years, before I finally decided it was the right time to retire her. She still had plenty of energy, but she was starting to feel unsound in her ridden work, so I felt it was time to stop work. In the week leading up to her death, she was galloping with excitement when I appeared at the gate to lead her in to her stable, and she was cantering in sideways. This was not a horse who was going to go quietly. Looking back, I am so glad she transitioned the way she did. A slow, lingering illness would not have suited her at all. Making her exit whilst dancing and prancing was the way to go. This was a horse who truly knew how to live and die – letting those wings take her to her final destination.

Tiffany was a true gift. To even have one horse like this in your life is beyond lucky, so I decided it wasn't something I would try to repeat. My next horse, I decided, would be loved in their own right; there would be no comparison to Tiffany. Once again, I fancied a young horse, who needed bringing on, ideally a long-term project. Although I am no longer interested in competing, I still love challenges, so buying a horse to just get on and go would not suit me at all.

After Tiffany's death, I was not in a rush to buy another horse. I decided that when the time was right, the horse would find me. I would not go looking for it. In the meantime, there was an overweight Gypsy Vanner mare on the yard who needed to get slimmer and fitter. I offered to exercise her for the owner, and so this is what I did for the next few months. She was a very sweet horse, but way too straightforward for me. Nevertheless, I enjoyed the process of getting her fit, and lots of riding out increased her confidence no end.

During this time, a friend on the yard kept showing me pictures of a dark grey 16hh thoroughbred mare. The horse belonged to a friend of hers and she was up for sale. At nine years old, she was older than what I wanted. Added to this, the photos weren't really grabbing me. I felt neutral about her.

Then she showed me pictures of another horse, a bay thoroughbred/new forest gelding. He was also 9 years old, but there was something about this horse that did get to me. He had a really kind, sensitive looking eye. This was a horse I had to go and see. To cut a long story short, I was all set to buy him, but then he failed the vetting. I had promised myself that if he failed, I would walk away. And so, it was. Disappointed, and suddenly desperate for a horse, I agreed to go and look at the grey mare. After all, it wouldn't hurt to have a look.

**Jazz**

My first impressions of Jazz were certainly not along the lines of *"Wow, she is amazing. I must have her!"* But there was something about her that touched my heart. She was very pretty, and there was a real sweetness and vulnerability about her. I wasn't so impressed by how she was standing. Resting a hind leg and pointing her diagonal front foot, I wondered about leg or back issues. Other times, she even appeared to be resting a front foot. *"Let's see how she rides"* I thought to myself.

I watched her owner ride her first. She was a good rider (better than me), riding her very sympathetically and gently. She rode sound, so my worries at how she had been standing were unfounded, but she did appear to dish very slightly, and around circles she had a tendency to fall out. Nevertheless, something was catching in my throat. There was a real quality to her paces, and I loved her energy and sensitivity. This horse was without doubt the sort I am drawn to.

A month later, this beautiful, sensitive soul arrived at our yard. Even from the very first, I could sense something deeply spiritual about her. As she stood on the trailer, her head turned, and her eyes met mine. As I looked into the ancient, spiritual wisdom staring back at me, I knew this horse was going to be unlike any I had encountered before. It is absolutely no coincidence that this spiritual horse arrived in my life, just as I was entering my spiritual phase.

In the years that have followed, I am humbled by the many lessons this amazing horse has taught me. She has really shaped me and helped me grow into the person I am today. More than anything, she has made me realise we have a long way to go to truly understand the nature of horses and to work with them in a respectful way.

Jazz has proven to be a very complex horse, but for me this is a sign of her high intelligence. In many ways, she is a contradiction of opposites. At times, she can come across as quite bossy and opinionated – with people and other horses alike. But at other times, she has seemed very scared and vulnerable. Seeing this side of her, makes me realise the bossiness is a bit of a front. There is an incredible sweetness about her, and she has beautiful manners. She is also very engaging, particularly with people she has never met before. She loves to introduce herself to new people, sniffing and kissing them, and this makes her very endearing.

She is expert at working her way into people's hearts. Only this week, a vet spent a couple of hours with me after an attack of colic. After giving her a gut relaxant and a full rectal examination, it was found that she had a slightly twisted gut, so we spent time lunging her, with periods of rest in between. As is usual, Jazz was the perfect patient – sweet, compliant and understanding- knowing we were trying to help. The vet was bowled over by her, explaining that occasionally a horse really gets to her. As she confided the next day, Jazz was one of these horses. She had actually been up at 2.00am in the night, worrying about her.

At other times, she can seem grumpy and bad-tempered. I now recognise this grumpiness as a means of expressing information and I see it as a very valuable tool. It is great that Jazz feels comfortable enough to be able to express herself, and always, it is an indication for me to listen.

It was clear very early on, that Jazz had physical and emotional/mental issues. Although fine to hack out, there were moments when her adrenaline would completely overthrow her. At these times, she would leap in the air, like a bouncy Tigger. Luckily, these outbursts only happened three times in the first three months, and although it wasn't as bad as bucking, rearing or bolting, she did keep up the leaping in the air on all four feet until we arrived back at the yard. Although, she was generally quiet and well behaved to handle, there were times when she would be transfixed by something, rigid with fear and rooted to the spot. She would get quite upset – increased heartbeat, tearing around in circles- although this was fairly infrequent. But it was stabling her that was the worst. On the yard I was on then, the horses had to come in at night from 1 November until 1 April. Although most of the time she was fine, every couple of weeks, she would be really upset about being in, weaving and box-walking. At these times, I was at a loss to understand why. The other horses would be in, and I could not see what was upsetting her. As soon as you led her out of the stable, she would be fine again.

There were also issues in the ménage. Although happy to work in there, she would often resort to headshaking and she often rushed through her paces, unbalancing herself. In canter particularly, she would hollow, throwing her head up, and be very stressed, bouncy and lacking rhythm. Her ears would pin back in anger if I asked for canter, and there were moments when she would feel furious. At her worst, you only had to think about cantering, and she would either take her energy away from you, or she would just refuse to move. To her credit, she never attempted to dislodge me. At times, it was even hard to get her to walk or to stand. She would just jog.

This was fine. I had bought her as a long-term project, and so it was pretty much as I expected. What I didn't expect, was that after two years of schooling and lunging, we were probably in a worse place than when we had started. We seemed to be going backwards. She was far too sensitive to have lessons with instructors. It would be too fast paced, and for me, it would feel forceful and unyielding. It just wasn't in alignment with how I felt it should be.

To help with Jazz's issues, I started experimenting with healing. I became Reiki attuned and used it regularly on Jazz. There was clearly a shift in her mental wellbeing. She started to relax and her canter work in the school became less crazy. We even did a little jumping, and although a bit on the fast side, we were both enjoying it. Although the Reiki worked well for her stable issues when I was with her, I wasn't always around when she was upset. Finally, the fourth year that she came in, the solution came to me, and it went on to work like a complete dream. I used Reiki to cleanse the stable, before bringing her in for the winter. The results were amazing. In the three years following this, I only witnessed her get upset on the very odd occasion, and it was very mild; just the slightest bit of weaving, and she got over it very quickly. I was expecting to do regular top-ups, but it proved to not be the case.

Then, towards the beginning of 2019, I moved yards. The first night of coming in her stable, she was a bit unsettled. As on the previous yard, I used Reiki to give the stable a thorough clean. My jaw dropped when I saw how quickly it worked. Within 40 minutes, Jazz was fast asleep with her eyes tight shut. I could barely believe how my horse had gone from so wound up to relaxed and fast asleep, in such a short space of time. It just didn't seem possible! From that moment on, Jazz just loved her stable, and for the first time in the seven years I had owned her, she chose to be in her stable during the day in the summer. Weaving had become a thing of the past.

The biggest lesson that Jazz taught me is this: the more challenging your horse, the greater the teacher they are. For those of you who have such a horse, please be immensely grateful. If you weren't ready for such a challenge, this horse would not be in your life. The lessons these horses teach us, can take us way beyond horsemanship skills. These horses can evolve our very souls. We just need to step back and look from an eagle's perspective what lessons these horses are trying to get across. Is there something within ourselves that we need to work on?

In my case, it was my ego. I have never considered myself egotistic, but Jazz has really highlighted to me just how far my ego was running the show. She has reminded me of the thoughts I had in my head, when she first came into my life. Having trained my last two horses into perfect role models, and allowing them to reach their full potential, I had the same plans for Jazz. As with my first two horses, I imagined it to be really straightforward. We would hack out to teach relaxation, and then I would gently start to introduce schooling and lunging. I expected this "fixing" of my horse to be much quicker than the other two. After all, I now had nearly forty years of riding/ handling horses under my belt, and now I was on my spiritual journey. I understood so much about finding inner calm and mindfulness thinking. I wanted to prove to those people who had said *"You will never get that horse right"* that any horse can be mended and made good.

I now understand the errors in thinking this way. *"Why do I need fixing? Can't you just accept me as I am? I accept you as you are"* my horse points out. What is it with the human brain – why do we always need to be doing, thinking, planning, fixing? Why can't we just be? Accept things as they are and enjoy whatever is presenting itself. Just being, instead of doing! Ok, I see this now. Enjoying the moment, without trying to control outcomes or trying to run the show is making a huge difference in how my horse works with me. Now, I let her have as much say in what we do and what speed we go at. She has as much right to enjoy the ride as I do. Compromise is the key to any good relationship, and it makes no difference whether this is a human relationship or a human/animal relationship. The same rules still apply.

The final lesson in taming my ego arose when I was prepared to listen to my horse. That voice which I heard, telling me to put aside riding/training ambitions and to concentrate on our healing potential, was the soul voice of my horse, expressing her deepest wishes and ambitions. Finally, I was prepared to hear – through my heart, not my mind. In listening to her and in really trying to fulfil her soul purpose, there has been an incredible shift, not just in my horse's demeanour, but in our relationship. From the moment I put pen to paper, her grumpiness just seemed to evaporate. Our relationship seemed much deeper. She would frequently talk to me with little nickers. She would come cantering up the field to me and give huge neighs when hearing the sound of my car entering the yard. We are connecting on a much deeper level and with this connection comes harmony and flow.

I am not trying to beat myself up too much. I think ego is a big obstacle for a lot of riders. From the moment we first sit in the saddle, we are trained to get the horse doing what we want, at the pace we choose. Our horsemanship skills are judged by how obedient, well-mannered and well-schooled our horses appear. What we fail to notice is how shutdown and resigned some of these horses actually are. They just feel defeated, because they have no voice. They are a slave to our wishes and ambitions. The idea that our horse may have his own purpose for being here would probably be scorned by the vast majority of riders, who still believe that horses were put on Earth to serve mankind. They would not even consider they may be here to further mankind.

Jazz has helped mirror a lot of things for me. *"It is all very well you trying to straighten and supple me; but what about yourself? How fit and supple are you?"* Yes, she was right. My riding needed a lot of work, and my crookedness and stiffness was just exacerbating our problems. This last couple of years, I have worked with a rider biomechanics teacher, and sorting my riding issues has helped resolve a lot of Jazz's physical issues. More recently, I have also taken up daily yoga and a rider fitness program, which has benefitted my riding no end, resulting in a much more relaxed and balanced horse. In fact, as I am finalising the editing of this book, I can't quite believe the improvements we have made in our riding work. It is so easy to blame the horse, rather than taking a good, honest look at ourselves.

So, eight years on, we have come a long way. I have loved the journey and how much it has taught me. I now realise that to establish a true partnering of the horse, we have to be prepared to listen, even if it is to face up to our own flaws and imperfections. But, in so doing, we can become not only better horsemen, but also better people. I have no doubt that there are still many lessons for me to learn, but now I am the listening and willing student, hopefully I will progress a bit quicker.

## My Daughter's Lessons

My daughter has been the guardian of two ponies in her life. Both ponies had very similar lessons for her, and I am very grateful to both of them.

Lauren, my daughter, has always been highly driven, a trait that neither me nor her dad ever possessed. From the moment she was very young, she has been extremely conscientious and ambitious. Whereas most parents have to encourage their children to do homework, I would be asking Lauren to give it a break. I had nightmares of her suffering a nervous breakdown by the time she was a teenager. Failure was not an option for Lauren. Everything she did, her effort was 100% and she was successful in every endeavour; at least, everything that involved her own input.

This is where the ponies came to my rescue. They taught her a very valuable lesson indeed – that it is ok to fail. When things go wrong, the world isn't going to end, and it is not going to come crashing around your feet. You just pick yourself up and you try again.

As was typical with Lauren, she worked very hard with her ponies to get them well-schooled, supple and able. Both ponies could be super-talented when they put their mind to it. Chelsea, her first pony, was a really good jumper. But at fifteen and having spent all her life doing pony club and competitions, there were days when she just wasn't in the mood for it. So, although she won many first prizes at shows, there were some days when she would say *"Not today"* and would be eliminated by refusing to jump the fences. Sometimes when she did this, Lauren would just let it sail over her head, suffering the humiliation that all riders are initiated into.

Silver too, had the same lessons to teach her. She worked hard at bringing his schooling to a level where he could compete. He proved to be particularly good at dressage, winning a lot of competitions. But, as with Chelsea, there were days when he wouldn't focus and would be really spooky, making it very difficult to ride an accurate dressage test. *"They are not machines"* I would tell her. *"They have off days just like we do. Accept what you are given."*

So, from the age of ten, when Chelsea came into her life, Lauren learned that failure can be as beneficial as success. It brings you down-to-earth, and really makes you appreciate the days when things go well, and you are successful. Those winning days are not taken for granted. By experiencing failure, you learn the value of success. More importantly, by losing the fear of failure, you can fully relax and enjoy the moment. And Lauren does now. She absolutely loves competing, but nowadays it is for the thrill and enjoyment, rather than for the winning. Best of all, she has learned to be more relaxed about her work. She sailed through her GCSE'S and A Levels with a smile on her face. There was no anxiety or panic, the same with her veterinary degree. She is now a vet in a small animal practise and is loving it.

**Horses Highlighting Our Issues**

There are instances where a person has repeatedly sold and bought horses, only to find that the same problem occurs with each and every one. This is a lesson which is crying out to be addressed.

Recently, someone told me about a woman they knew who was in this very situation. She lacked confidence when hacking out, and so she bought a supposedly bomb-proof horse. However, the horse proved not to be as advertised, so she sold it on. A lot of time and effort was spent, in ensuring that the next horse was safe and non-spooky. Everything was fine for a time, but then that horse started to spook as well, so he was sent on his way. This set up a pattern and these problems kept repeating with every horse she bought.

Those horses were acting as a mirror, reflecting back to the woman her own insecurities and lack of confidence. Clearly, this woman was refusing to accept that it wasn't the horses that had a problem; it was herself. She needed to recognise that the horse takes confidence from the rider, not the other way round. There are some amazing horses out there who will happily carry a nervous rider and not be affected by their energy, but there are more horses who look to the rider for confidence. This woman would have been better off taking herself to a riding establishment, where she could learn to gain confidence under expert tuition.

**Intuition**

With all the horses in my life, I have recognised that intuition/gut feeling led me to take them on. In all cases, this was the over-riding reason for them coming into my life. And I am not unique in this. Time and again, people tell me how they believe they were chosen by their horse, and they felt an inexplicable connection with them. I find this quite interesting, as this is not something that is typically included in a *"What to Look for When Buying a Horse"* list. To be honest, if I had been using my logical thinking, knowledgeable brain, I would have walked away from all three of the horses I bought for myself. Thank goodness I trusted the feelings of my heart. This is an important lesson in itself: emotional intelligence is not something to be ignored. It can be more valuable than our brain.

In the resulting chapters, I look more closely at the nature of the horse. By having a more in-depth understanding of the horse, we can develop more empathy and compassion towards him, creating a deeper horse/human bond overall.

## Chapter 7 – The Prey Horse

*The horse is very much a mirror,*
*Reflecting all our mental and physical imbalances.*

As any horse-lover is aware, there is one huge difference between horses and man. Whereas humans are at the top of the food chain, the horse is not. There is always the chance they may be another animal's dinner – and not just that of an animal. Some countries today still have horsemeat on their menus. And even here in the UK, there have been media stories claiming that horsemeat has been used in burgers.

In spite of thousands of years of domestication, the prey instinct is still very much part of a horse's nature. It may be impossible to alleviate it altogether, even though the threat to horses in the modern world is considerably less than in times long gone. And maybe this is a good thing and the way it should be, for this instinct drives horses and influences them in many ways, e.g., it is a big motivation in racehorses to run as part of the herd.

The prey instinct in the horse means that he is adept at reading the intentions of others towards him. It is said that a group of wild horses can not only sense if a lion is in their environment and close by, but they can also sense the intention of the lion. People who have hung out with these herds reckon that the horses instinctively know whether or not the lion is eyeing them up for his next meal. If so, the flight instinct kicks in, and they will make themselves scarce very quickly. On the other hand, if they detect the lion has a full stomach, then they appear to be completely nonchalant about the lion's presence. It is not very clear how the horse is picking this information up, but it is generally perceived to be an intuitive, sixth sense ability.

There does appear to be retained traits of this ability in the domesticated horse, as some horses do seem to be very perceptive in picking up their human's intention towards them. For instance, I have witnessed some horses reacting unfavourably to a vet approaching them from the other side of the barn.

Due to the prey horse mentality, horses do experience the world very differently to us humans, and we need to appreciate this much more than we do. We need to be far more understanding, compassionate and patient towards our horse's fears. More than anything, we need to realise that when our horses resist or "play-up", it is not out of naughtiness; it is an instinctual response to either pain or fear. Throughout the rest of the chapter, I have categorised some of the biggest problems that people have with their horses, all which relate to the prey horse mentality.

**Inability to Ride Out on Own**

This can be a big ask for a lot of horses. Being naturally gregarious, it is natural for horses to want to be around others of their kind. Added to this, there is safety in numbers! Taking them away from other horses can be a difficult thing. It takes a lot of confidence on the horse's part, together with trust in the rider, to achieve a ride out on your own. Many horses can be trained to do this. As with anything involving horses, it is a case of being patient and just asking for a little bit at a time, gradually building up. Just leading a horse out for short stints would be enough to start with, because at least he can see his handler, and this will give him more confidence.

All three of my horses have been very different. Smokey, my first pony, despite being highly spooky, would happily ride out on his own and also lead the way if he was with other horses. However, he was far less spooky when ridden behind other horses, because he was able to switch off from the role of having to warn them of danger.

Tiffany preferred being a lead horse or riding out on her own. Jazz is much more complex. When riding out with others, she was generally happy to lead, but there were places at our last yard (certain houses or the gate across the road) where she would ask to have a lead past. Riding on our own, there were places she wouldn't go past at all, which meant that some rides were out of bounds for us. I could never understand the reasons and put it down to these places emitting energies she was uncomfortable with.

We moved yards in March 2019, and thankfully nothing on the new yard is out of bounds for us, so we mostly ride out on our own.

**General Spookiness**

It is rare to find a horse that is totally 100% bomb proof. If a horse is to survive in the wild, he needs his senses and instincts to be as sharp as they can possibly be. Those that lack the quick-fire reactions are more likely to end up on someone's dinner plate. Those instincts and senses are still very much intact, and in good working order, even today.

That sudden movement may cause the horse to shoot sideways, as he evaluates whether he needs to take flight.

The senses of a horse are very different to our human senses. As prey animals, the eyes are on the side of their head, allowing them to take advantage of an almost 360 degrees vision. So, sight wise, they can take in far more than us humans. The only blind spots are directly behind and directly in front of the horse, which explains why some horses react badly to noises behind them, when they can't see the source of the noise.

Also, horses are much more sensitive to light. A horse has excellent night vision yet struggles slightly to see clearly in bright sunlight. They can become easily spooked if asked to go from a light, sunny area into a dark area, as they are temporarily blinded. If you ever watch badminton on the TV, you will recall the difficulty some horses experience going from the bright light into a dark spinney. It can also create problems if you are trying to load a horse into a dark trailer or stable.

Jazz asks whether I have noticed her aversion to bright sunlight. Yes, I had noted that she can be far spookier on bright, sunny days. This is why, she tells me. Her eyes struggle to adjust to the light/ dark contrasts. Riding down bridle paths with trees running either side are particularly problematic as the contrasts are so much more acute.

Horses' hearing is way more sensitive than ours. They can pick up a higher range of sound that is inaudible to us, and they can hear sounds from further away, so we may not even be aware of them.

Horses are also brilliant at sensing emotion behind the human voice. Any change in pitch or slight wavering of the intonation will be detected and possibly translated into a message that you don't feel safe or in control.

Horses are also able to associate some individual sounds with a positive or negative memory. The sound of a hunting horn can have a very excitable effect on a lot of horses who are familiar with the sound.

Like dogs, the sense of smell in the horse is very acute, but unlike dogs, it is not their primary sense. Nevertheless, smells can trigger an emotional response in the horse. Their acute sense of smell also means they can pick up on our emotions. We transmit anxiety, anger or negativity through the release of pheromones. This can make it particularly problematic if we suffer nerves when competing, as the horse will literally be able to smell our fear. No wonder we witness so many nervous/tense horses at shows.

So, due to horses having much more heightened senses than we do, it is natural that they pick up a lot more that is going on in their environment and respond to it accordingly. Often these responses will trigger the fight/flight response.

My experiences have taught me that horses have an absolutely brilliant visual memory, so their ability to map out their environment can resort in spookiness when objects are placed differently. On our yard, the jumping poles and wings are placed just outside the ménage. My friend's horse would become wildly spooky if any of these things moved or were placed in a different way.

My first pony, Smokey, really amazed me with his superb ability to map things. We often crossed a busy main road, riding up a wide pathway that ran alongside a petrol station. At the side of the petrol station was a large metal box. We had passed this box quite happily for years, but then one day, I was attempting to cross the road when Smokey started running backwards in goggle mode. I managed to get him moving forward and crossed the road, realising it was the big box he was spooking at. It was only when we were a few feet away that I noticed that the box had moved backwards by about a foot. This was why Smokey was spooking. I was in absolute awe that this pony had picked up the fact this box had moved when we had been at least 80 feet away. I couldn't even comprehend how this was possible. But Smokey never left you in any doubt what he was spooking at. With him, the reason was always obvious.

Another important thing to note with spookiness is that the brain works differently, depending on which eye the horse is seeing the object with. This explains why a lot of horses will not react at all if they are passing an object and seeing it through their left eye, but then react when they are coming the other way and see it through the right eye. As we see through both eyes simultaneously, we don't experience this problem, so find it hard to understand why the horse reacts so differently.

An interesting thing with spookiness is that each horse is unique, and will not only react differently, but will react to very different things. Jazz doesn't like drains and other animals, and she can also get upset by people walking in the distance where half their body is hidden by the hedge, giving the impression that their head is walking along the hedge. Clearly a vivid imagination at work here! Also, she dislikes logs suddenly making an appearance – things to be viewed with high suspicion. Sometimes, I just don't know; in these instances, I assume it is an energy thing, and she is picking up some vibration that is outside my awareness.

Strangely, she is way less spooky when she is riding in a new place. Her interest in a new and different environment overrides any anxiety, and she is not being bored and looking for things to spook at. Also, she hasn't mapped her environment, so she can't react to things that have changed in some way. Despite this, she has total confidence with poles, jumps and fillers, never showing a slight reaction to any of them. Silver on the other hand, is rarely spooky on a ride, but in the arena, he can be highly suspicious of poles on the ground (he is fine if they are presented as a jump) and fillers.

It is claimed that the rider's confidence or lack of it, can also affect the level of a horse's spookiness. I can see how this works; if the rider is tense and anxious, then the horse will certainly feel this, and it may cause him to feel the same way. This is more typical with a green and inexperienced horse. However, as proven with my experience with Smokey, not all spookiness is caused by a rider's fears. Although he did improve with time, he did retain some element of spookiness, despite my sister and I being very confident riders.

When our horses are spooking, it is vital that we don't react. Those riders who shout and smack their horses are just creating future problems. All it does is create more tension and anxiety in the horse, exacerbating their fears and giving them even more reason to be scared. I just gently encourage Jazz on. If she resists, I just sit there, talking soothingly to her, waiting until she is happy to pass the object. Giving her plenty of time to check out the object and allowing her to relax is the easiest and most successful way of getting her to pass it.

Occasionally, there are times when the waiting game doesn't work, and I relate one such incident here. I was riding towards the yard (only a few minutes away) when we approached a house that Jazz is always very tense about passing. Funnily enough, she has no tension passing it going away from home with her left eye on it but passing it with the right eye is a different matter.

As we walked down the hill towards it, some horses in a neighbouring field started galloping up the hill away from the house. Instantly, Jazz was on high alert. What had scared them? The answer for her was obvious. There were some brightly coloured dome shaped tents in the back garden of this house, and they could just be detected through the trees. Taking all this in was enough for Jazz to imitate a statue. Stock still, head in air with nostrils flaring, Jazz was not going to walk down this hill. I stood for a couple of minutes, but as she was starting to edge more and more into the middle of the road, it was clear this wasn't the safest strategy.

So, I decided to offer Jazz a choice. We could turn back and go the long way home (20 minutes instead of a few minutes) or we could pass the scary objects. I turned Jazz around and she happily trotted up the road. That is until we crossed the brow of the hill. You could literally hear the penny drop in Jazz's brain – this way would take a lot longer. She stopped dead, weighing up the options. Another half a minute and she was making it clear that she was not going to take another step in this opposite direction. So once again I calmly turned her around, heading back towards the scary tents. This time she knew what she had to do. The choices had been made very clear to her and she had decided. She didn't stop once. Yes, she was tense and like a coiled spring, but we passed the house without any adverse reaction. I was pleased with Jazz and how she had processed it and made the right choice. It is a very valuable exercise when the horse learns to figure things out for himself, and much more productive than battling with the horse, which only creates distrust and disharmony.

**Fear of Water**

This is a very common fear, but I don't think people truly appreciate why so many horses are afraid of walking through water. Again, it is down to the prey instinct. For the horse, there could be a crocodile or some other nasty creature lurking in those muddy waters.

Jazz highlighted this concern to me not long after she had appeared in my life. We were riding through some very large woods and there were a lot of huge, muddy puddles. Poor Jazz stood in front of them, literally shaking from head to toe. I could feel her fear, and I really, really felt for her. The muddy water obscures the horse's vision. They aren't to know that there isn't some monster lurking in there, waiting to pounce when an unsuspecting horse walks through. These instinctual fears are buried deep within the horse's psyche. All they need us to do is to understand and to respond appropriately.

My reaction was to stroke Jazz's neck, talking to her soothingly. I let her watch Silver walk forwards and backwards through the water, taking my time until she felt relaxed enough to follow him through. The important thing is to feel calm yourself – don't let your horse's anxiety affect your piece of mind. It is important that at least one half of the partnership feels relaxed, helping to transfer these feelings to the other half. Don't feel rushed either. Just be prepared to take as much time as you need.

During the rest of that ride, we just sought out as many puddles as possible, and let Jazz follow Silver through them. By the time we left the woods, Jazz was confidently walking through them in front. I can honestly say that this approach worked beautifully. We have never had a problem with water since. Even when we are trotting along a road on our own and we encounter a 100ft length flood on the road in front of us, there is no hesitation in her gait. She is the same with water on cross-country courses – she will happily trot or canter through them.

I can't emphasise how important it is to empathise with your horse, reassuring him as much as possible. The slightest bit of impatience and scolding on your part could set up problems with water for a long time to come. By yelling, shouting and being forceful with your horse, you are creating bad associations with water.

**Fear of Ditches**

Again, this is a very similar problem to the water. Most horses fear ditches because they can't see what is inside of them. They make a great hiding place for a predator to jump out and attack them.

As with the water, it is important for the rider to understand and empathise with the horse's fear. Any negative reaction on your part is just going to exacerbate your horse's fear and create a bad association with the ditch.

When Lauren was about twelve, she took part in an instructional rally on a cross-country course. There was a lovely young horse, about four years old, who was in her group, and he had very little experience of cross-country jumping. He had gone really well in the session, jumping everything that was asked of him. That is until they came to the ditch. Frightened, he started backing off, and the more he resisted, the angrier his teenage rider became, hitting and screaming at him.

Witnessing his reaction (as well as the rider who had no self-control), the instructor should have called it a day – after all this was a young horse was probably physically and mentally exhausted by this time. Unfortunately, the battle continued for a good 15 minutes, when the tearful rider finally admitted defeat.

This scenario haunted me for a long time afterwards. It only takes 15 minutes to ruin a good horse for life – setting up the mental barriers that would take an incredibly patient and understanding rider to dismantle. Sadly, there are not enough of these riders around, so I am not optimistic that this horse ever went on to conquer his fear of ditches. I heard shortly after that the rider had sold him on, after creating goodness knows how many more mental fears in that beautiful horse.

Jazz had no previous experience of cross-country riding or ditches before she came into my life, so I started her off gently, letting her see Silver jumping them. Then we started with very shallow ditches, building up gradually from there. Taking the process slowly has paid dividends, and she has never shown any hesitation in approaching or jumping ditches.

As with everything to do with horses, patience and time are the keywords. As long as the process is taken slowly and without force, you are setting up confidence in the horse that can help create real progress. Eventually, you will have a horse that enjoys the challenges of jumping ditches.

**Fear of Other Animals**

This has been a biggie with Jazz. The first day she arrived, I turned her out in her new field. She took no notice of the other horses – she was oblivious to them. Not so with the cows, who were a few fields away. Her head high, nostrils flaring, she stood stock still and rigid, every sinew and every nerve alive and on fire, her eyes fixed unwaveringly on those distant cows. Interspersed with staring rigidly at them, she would take herself off for a trot or gallop around the field, before coming once again to a standstill, returning to stare wildly at those cows and trying to assimilate whether they were friend or foe. This pattern continued for the next couple of hours. It made not a scrap of difference that all the horses around her were grazing quietly and contentedly. She was just locked into the fear of her own wild imaginings.

About two months later, I had a worse encounter with some pigs. I was out riding on my own, when I spotted some pigs in front and to the right of us on the lane. They were in an outside enclosure, and although we had passed them many times before, this was the first time they were actually in view. Not only were they in full view, but to make matters worse, they were grunting. Although we were about 100 feet away from them, Jazz stopped dead. She started snorting, her heart beating so hard I could feel the pounding through my boots. I realised very quickly, that I needed to turn back and make a quick exit, but it wasn't going to be easy. In between the standing, she would turn sharply in circles, before stopping to stare at the pigs. She wanted to get away from them, but was afraid to turn her back on them, terrified that they might be planning an attack.

As she wheeled in circles, I felt my saddle starting to tip. I had failed to sufficiently tighten the girth. A super-fast dismount on my part followed, but the idea that I may calm her quicker on the ground failed to materialise. She was completely oblivious to my presence; even a kind lady appearing with some nuts in a bucket failed to impress even the remotest interest.

I realised with horror that I was not going to calm my horse. In fact, she was getting increasingly agitated. The only option left was to try and head home with her whirling around me in circles. So, that is what we did. I had a road to negotiate, so while my horse careered in circles around me, the traffic was forced to a standstill. That mile home was the longest mile of my life. Finally, we made it through the gates of the yard, and in that instance, my horse's adrenaline dropped faster than a brick. The relief was so immense I didn't even try to suppress the tears coursing down my face. It was a miracle we had made it home in one piece without anyone being hurt.

Needless to say, I avoided that ride for a while, until a couple of months later, I learned that the pigs had been sold. However, that ride was still out of bounds for us when out on our own as it had plenty of new residents – hens, ducks, goats, miniature ponies, donkeys and mules – none of which Jazz was impressed by. She would happily ride along there behind Silver, but I had learned my lesson.

A lot of horses seem to fear pigs, possibly because they are closely related to boars who preyed on horses many years ago. Years of domestication and controlled breeding has failed to wipe out those survival instincts, which have been carried through from generation to generation. At some level, the strong smell of pigs still awakens that deep fear within horses; an ancestral memory that triggers the flight/fight response.

Although nothing comes close to her reaction to the pigs, Jazz is highly suspicious of a lot of animals. With cows and sheep, it is generally when they suddenly appear in a new field. Once she has passed them in that field, she is fine thereafter. She really dislikes donkeys, not quite as badly as pigs. The reason for this, she tells me, is because she had never seen them before she came to me. Animals they see infrequently, including deer, can freak them out because they don't know which animals are predator or prey, so they don't know how that animal is going to react to them.

Surprisingly, most horses seem quite happy with dogs. This is because they commonly see dogs, including around the yard with humans. Horses know that the humans they trust and rely on wouldn't bring them in to the horse's space if they were going to attack them. It is all a matter of trust. The times the horses do react to dogs are when they are running around snapping at their heels. When a dog acts in this aggressive manner, it is no surprise that the horse is upset.

**Trailer or Box Loading**

The prey instinct in horses can make trailer loading very difficult, and I don't think we really appreciate how much we ask for the horse to load calmly and obediently.

Horses prefer wide open spaces where they can both see and flee from a perceived threat. So, asking them to walk up the ramp of a trailer and then confining them between narrow partitions can be extremely stressful for them, as they are likely to feel trapped and claustrophobic. Not only that, but a trailer is also a big, scary object, which makes a noise and wobbles when you step on it. The light can also be very dim in a trailer, meaning the horse's eyes have to adjust from the light to the dark. When you start moving, it can be very difficult for them to balance.

As with anything, the key to loading successfully is time and patience. It is particularly important that the horse is happy just standing on the trailer before you even attempt to move. So, lots of practise, when you have time on your hands and you are not going to get frustrated, is a necessity. The horse needs to be able to associate the trailer with good things – like treats, fuss, praise and scratches, not negative things, like shouting, anger and force. As soon as the horse feels any pressure from the handler, he is naturally going to resist.

I once witnessed an attempt to load a very small show pony on to a trailer, and it was a brilliant demonstration of how not to attempt it, followed by a much more correct method. It is no surprise to note that the failed attempt involved three adults (including two men). They were literally attempting to virtually carry this pony onto the trailer. And naturally, he was resisting the pressure. He would get to the top of the ramp, rear, and come over the side. Eventually, failing to make any progress, frustrated and red in the face, they walked off, deciding to calm their frazzled tempers with a cup of tea. A very young girl, about 8 years old, was left holding the pony. Very calmly and gently, she talked to the pony, asking him to take a step up the ramp, before stopping to praise and pat him. She inserted no pressure whatsoever – there was no pulling, and her body language was very soft. There was an air of complete calm about this girl, and it was clear that she totally understood this pony's fear. By the time the adults returned, the pony was happily standing on the trailer, munching his hay. I was hypnotised by the whole performance, recognising that children often have a much more natural, understanding and empathic way with horses than us adults.

**Breed of Horse**

The breed of horse can very much influence the level of spookiness. Some breeds are without doubt generally more docile, easy-going and calmer. Certain bloodlines have followed rigorous breeding programs, the intention being to produce calm, easy trainable horses. Conversely, thoroughbreds and Arabs are renowned for their hot-blooded nature. Arabs were originally bred to be vigilant, as their owners were subject to ambush, so a watchful, reactive horse was a good thing. Thoroughbreds have been bred for speed, so the enhancement of the flight instinct also means that they are generally spookier.

I have heard it claimed from those people who are part of the mounted police that the mixed breed horses are generally the easiest to get through sensory training. They claim that the "hot breeds" such as Arabs and thoroughbreds, can present real challenges.

The general rule of thumb seems to be that the finer boned the horse, the higher its fear levels. I do have to say though that there are exceptions to every rule. I have known some extremely calm, laid-back thoroughbreds, and some very spooky Heinz 57's. As I described in an earlier chapter, Smokey who was Connemara/Welsh cob, was one of the spookiest horses I have ever come across. Tiffany, on the other hand, who was extremely fine boned and possibly three-quarters thoroughbred, was the most bomb proof horse I have encountered. So, it isn't all down to breeding. Other factors, such as life experiences, confidence of the handler, and feeding, all have to be taken into account.

**Bonded Trust**

I do believe that over time, once your horse has established a good bond with you, he will become less spooky. This has certainly been the case with my horses.

Only this week whilst typing this, I have had a couple of beautiful experiences with Jazz, highlighting how strong our bond is and how much trust she has developed in me. In the one instance, Jazz was tied up by her stable. The owner of the yard wished to drop a big round bale of hay on the pallet right behind her (only about six feet away), using his digger. He asked me if Jazz would be ok with it, and without even thinking, I said *"Yes."* I guess it also shows how much confidence I have in her too. Jazz turned her head to have a look, but there was absolutely no tension in her body whatsoever and her eyes continued to gaze with a soft, interested look. After he went, somebody on the yard came over to me, exclaiming they couldn't believe how chilled my horse was. I could only agree. Later in the day, bringing her in from the field, as we walked down the track, we came face to face with eight white bags of ragwort. Jazz stopped, staring at them intently. She then nosed me forward as if to say, *"You go first, I will follow"* and then just quietly walked behind me. I just love it when you get to this level of trust. There is a real magic in the long-term bond of horse and handler.

The final thing to say is this: the horse has given us his mind, body and spirit in servitude to the human race. The least we can do in return is to understand and empathise with his fears. He is a prey animal after all. When you really stop and think, it is nothing short of a miracle that we are actually able to ride an animal that was born to be so fearful. All the horse asks in return is for us to understand and be patient. How can we refuse such a humble request?

# Chapter 8 – The Training/Riding Horse

*"You must dance to the rhythm of my song" insists Man.*
*"But only if your song is worthy of my dance" replies The Horse.*

Just because the horse has carried us for thousands of years doesn't mean it is right or something we should continue to do. More and more people are questioning the ethics of riding. Is it right to sit astride a beautiful, sentient animal, suppressing his spirit in the process? Is it right to have control over the mind and body of another, dominating him and insisting that he obey our commands? Doesn't this point towards a master/servant relationship?

For any person who truly loves horses, it is inevitable that at some point the mind has pondered these questions. I am no different. Having ridden for forty years, I have had to step back at times and consider whether this is really the right thing to do. But at the end of the day, we can only come to our way of thinking through our own experiences. It is these which shape us, creating our thoughts and beliefs.

So based on my experiences, my thinking goes along these lines: Like just about everything in life, riding is a neutrality which we paint and bring to life with our attitudes, beliefs and energy. In other words, just like everything, riding can be a positive experience for the horse, or it can be a negative one. It has the potential to impact greatly the physical, mental, and emotional wellbeing of the horse, but whether they are positive changes or negative has a lot to do with the person on their back.

Ask yourself this: when you ride your horse does it feel like a harmonious connection where you are both uplifted through your joyful interaction, or does it feel more like a battleground where you are each trying to impose your will over the other? For whatever you feel it to be, your horse is almost certain to be of the same opinion.

**Do Horses Enjoy Being Ridden?**

Obviously, this is a very important consideration, for if they don't enjoy it, then it can be much harder justifying it. Again, I think the responsibility lies with the rider. It is very much down to us to make it an enjoyable experience. Later in this chapter, I discuss the attributes which a good rider/trainer should possess to make the experience a positive one, and I also look at the physical/emotional/mental and spiritual blocks which may inhibit the enjoyment for the horse.

So, what have I learned from the horses in my life when it comes to a horse's attitude towards riding?

My days with Smokey were very carefree. We explored miles of tracks, woodlands and huge areas where you could ride off road for miles (in the days before they cultivated them and turned them into country Parks with designated bridlepaths). They were times of fun and adventure, and I have not the slightest doubt that our ponies felt the joy and freedom in our souls, reflecting these states back to us.

I can honestly say, hand on heart, that my next horse, Tiffany, just loved being ridden. And we had the huge blessing of riding together for twenty-six years. We both cherished and loved our long rides together; rides which connected us deeply and forged a union so deep that communicating on a telepathic level was an effortless process. She taught me how harmonious a riding partnership could be, and I felt supremely grateful for every joyful step she took. Having complete faith and trust in each other, witnessing every ride as a beautiful gift, is something that many riding partners find hard to achieve. I also have no doubt that my deep gratitude and love for her was picked up so easily when I was astride her, through our energies mingling together. I am convinced that this uplifted her considerably, keeping her fit and well up to her death when she was thirty-four.

Silver, Lauren's loan pony, also had some very clear lessons about riding. He absolutely adored galloping and jumping fences across country. The more exhilarating the better as far as this pony was concerned! As a result, he really enjoyed Hunter Trials and Fun Rides. So much so, that he only had to see the ramp of a horsebox or trailer down, and you could barely hold him back.

Silver also demonstrated how much pride horses take in their work. There is no doubt in my mind that some horses really do like having a job to do and they do take pride in performing well. As he trotted into the arena of a dressage competition, I would just gasp at his charisma and presence. He seemed transformed and barely recognisable. No wonder the judges loved him so!

So, over the years, my horses have proven to me that riding can have many benefits. It can help keep their body in good shape; it can help forge a deep connection; it can give them a sense of self-worth and purpose; and it can stimulate their minds and senses.

But I also recognised very early on that this isn't necessarily the same for all horses. Many horses have negative riding experiences which cause them to become either problematic, uncooperative or shutdown. After Tiffany transitioned, my belief that any horse could be taught to enjoy being ridden was about to be sorely tested.

## Jazz's Attitude to Riding

When Jazz came into my life, for the first time ever, I was presented with a horse who made it clear that she didn't particularly enjoy being ridden. When I asked Jazz for her perspective on riding, this is what she said (I have kept it in her own words): -

*"From the moment someone put their leg over my back I hated it. How dare they! What right had they to control my body? What right had they to control my mind? I am a free spirit, not a vehicle for someone's ego. It was hard to suppress my anger, but I learned early on that choice just did not come into it. My opinions were swept under the carpet and if I dared to express how I felt, then punishment was the natural response. Once that person was on my back, I was expected to suppress all my emotions and reactions. Free expression became a distant memory! I was no better treated than a machine.*

*Once I left the polo yard, things did improve. There were less demands, and I was carrying someone whose beautiful energy uplifted me and helped me feel good about myself.*

*Then with you, it was different again. Part of my soul agreement was that I needed to carry you. There were lessons you needed to learn which could only be passed on through a riding partnership. It didn't mean that I couldn't express my opinion. You allowed me free expression, something for which I am grateful for.*

*My grumpiness at being tacked up was my way of showing that this was not my choice, and it isn't what I would choose to do. I was asking you to rethink your ideas. How could you make it more enjoyable? How could you make me a willing participant?*

*The questions continued to be asked.*

*When I took my energy away from you at the mere thought of cantering in the ménage, I asked you to be more creative. How could you change the record? Your eventual answer (boy, it took a long time though for you to figure it out) was a good one. You started asking for a canter out of walk instead of trot, accompanied by flooding your body with joy, imagining that we were running into the sea.*

*When I fell in through my shoulders on the left-hand rein, I asked you to consider your position and crookedness. Am I the problem or you? Who is the crooked one here? Yes, you eventually started working on your own body instead of being fixated with mine. Doing a daily yoga and rider program did wonders!*

*When I rushed forwards through all my paces, I asked you to be more subtle with your aids. Why push with your legs when all you need to do is change your breathing? Yes, practising this through our groundwork first was a good idea because it was then easily transferrable to our riding.*

*When I froze on rides out because at what was in front of us, I asked you to consider alternative routes.*

*When I froze at things you couldn't see, I asked you to feel the unseen.*

*When I refused to co-operate with instructors, I asked you to trust yourself and to step into your own power.*

*When I progressed slowly, I asked you to look at the long-term goal.*

*When I became agitated, I asked you to consider your energy.*

*When you tried to fix me, I asked you to consider your ego.*

*When you were close to throwing in the towel, I asked where was your faith and perseverance? You learned there are always answers, but sometimes they are off the beaten track, lying in the deepest, undiscovered hole. Do not fear to walk where others have not walked before you, for that is where the greatest expansion lies.*

*Every question I asked of you, there was always an answer. Not always the right one mind you, but eventually you saw the light. You have been slow to train – stubborn and stuck in your limited, conditioned way of thinking, but at last, we are starting to make progress. You have pretty well ditched the ego, embraced new ways of being, and worked on your inner self, and those changes are mirrored by me. We are well on the way to a partnership which embodies compromise, compassion and empathy.*

*Just remember. The problem is never with the riding, only how you go about the riding! When you ditch the whips, spurs, legs and hands, and start to communicate through the mind, breath and energy, then we are heading towards a harmonious connection."*

Yes, Jazz had worked on me like no horse ever had. How amazing that she came into my life at the point I was open and ready to take this on board. As I read this for a final time, I am amazed how far we have come. Recently, I rode Jazz over to a jumping clinic. She was simply amazing and didn't put a foot out of place. It was all so effortless! My daughter has been competing her over the last year in dressage, show-jumping and combined training, and they are both thoroughly enjoying themselves. At every event, Jazz has been impeccably behaved and a joy to ride.

But more importantly, I now have a horse who is happy to be ridden. The moment I throw my leg over her, she walks jauntily off down the lane, ears pricked, keen and eager as to what lies ahead. And she really enjoys the regular pole clinics we have on the yard, as unsurprisingly she does enjoy working her brain and having something to think about. *"Yes, this isn't so bad after all"* I hear her say.

**Training Horses**

Many people who have horses recognise the importance of good training. Not only can schoolwork help with the fitness and suppleness of the horse, but it can help lighten the horse on his front, teaching him to carry more weight on his hindquarters. Through good, correct schooling, your horse can be transformed into one who is a joy to ride, and it can be hugely beneficial for their body, resulting in less injury. It is no different to us really. People who keep their bodies in good working shape, are able to keep going for longer.

Today, there are a good variety of training methods, and the internet has opened up many that were previously inaccessible.

There is a tendency for people to get attached to one particular method, forsaking all others. But in truth, every method has something in its favour otherwise it wouldn't have become popular in the first place. Horses, like humans, are all completely unique, so what is going to work well for one horse is not necessarily going to work for another. It is very important therefore to remain open-minded and flexible. With this in mind, in an ideal world, the human, if he is to be serious about riding and training horses, would take the time to learn about all the different methods. He could then take the best things away from each method of training, adapting them to each individual horse.

A great trainer/author, Mark Rashid, makes this very point in his excellent series of horse books. His methods of training are very much focused on understanding and compassion, and he makes it very clear that there is no need for dominance in the training of horses. He goes as far as to reject all training methods, claiming that it is all down to common sense and allowing the horse time to figure things out for himself. He argues that the horse is highly intelligent, picking up very quickly which behaviours give him a reward, and which make things harder. He will then adjust his behaviour accordingly.

In his book, *"Horses Never Lie"* he describes how he owned a trekking centre for a while. One of the horses had a nasty habit of taking off with his rider and returning back to the centre. He would be made to school in the arena for a bit, before being ridden to re-join the other horses. It didn't take him long to work out that this bad behaviour was creating much more work. He was better off just going along with the others.

I think as with all things, we have a tendency to over-complicate. Obviously, it depends on what you are trying to achieve with your horse, but like anything, it can be as simple or as complicated as you wish to make it. There is so much evidence to prove that children can be just as effective in bonding and training their horses as experienced adults. My story in the previous chapter, of the young child loading her pony, is proof of this. Monty Roberts himself was a young child when he was successfully breaking and training horses. Another child, Carolyn Resnick, proved hugely successful in bonding with some wild horses. She spent three summers with them, and by the third, she was riding the lead mare with no tack or any means of restraint. It was a bond built on total trust and respect. I believe that horses have a very natural rapport with children. This may be down to the fact that children are less goal-orientated than adults; they have natural vision and creativity, as well as being more loving, empathic, joyful, compassionate and generally relaxed.

One of the big obstacles to training successfully, as Jazz points out to me, is that we just assume that the horse knows what he is supposed to do. So, we put a jump up in the school for the horse to go over, but how is he supposed to understand this? For all he knows, he may be expected to just stop in front of it or go around it. Going over it may not be something he comprehends.

Jazz informs me that we should use other horses to demonstrate what is required much more than we do. Let the novice horse watch the more experienced horse jump the fence so he understands what is expected of him. This is what happens in a herd. Young horses learn by watching and copying their elders.

When we are out on a ride, with Jazz and Silver riding side by side, if Silver goes into a medium trot, then Jazz immediately does the same. But this is the only time she will perform this movement.

Interestingly, as I am typing this, I have just read about a trainer who very much believes in using experienced horses to demonstrate moves. When she is ready to teach the Spanish walk, she uses an experienced horse who performs it in front of the learning horse. The latter then picks it up naturally without having to be taught. He just starts copying.

After Jazz enlightened me with this fact, I did try it out on a horse that was refusing to load. We put down the front of the trailer and kept leading Silver (expert loader) up and out. It didn't take long at all for the other horse to follow suit, as he had learned by watching Silver that there was nothing to fear.

**My Experience with Training Jazz**

When Jazz first came into my life, I was finding it hard to transform her into the supple and athletic horse she had the potential to be. She was a highly sensitive horse, to such an extent that the traditional methods of training I had used previously just didn't seem to be cutting it. Through the eyes of my sensitive horse, these old methods just seemed forceful and one-sided. It wasn't that she was resisting or playing up; it was just that to me it didn't feel right. I felt it was too demanding and dictatorial, and this was creating a lot of tension in my horse. It felt the right time to seek out more holistic methods where I could address her crookedness and tension, but which would be gentle and conducive to the lovely bond we had created. More than anything, I was looking to create a true and equal partnership.

There was someone on my yard who was into Natural Horsemanship, and she had started training with a local man who claimed to be very holistic in his approach. I decided to join forces with her, so for the next year, every three weeks we would journey over to his yard and participate in his training program.

The training was broken down into various components: groundwork, lunging, in hand work, riding and liberty work. Each component has a systematic building up of gymnastic exercises which progresses the horse, helping to make him straighter, suppler, lighter on the forehand, and teaching him to carry more weight on his quarters. I liked the idea that it was a slow and natural progression, enabling the horses mind and body to adjust over time, without demanding instant changes that the horse may find difficult to accommodate.

Although I was learning an awful lot through this way of training, I really didn't enjoy the lessons. More importantly, neither did Jazz! Although the exercises in themselves were very gentle, the trainer was intimidating in his approach. He used a pressure and release system for getting his message across, but I learned that, although this may be very effective for a lot of horses, it really is not ideal for a sensitive horse. Jazz is a horse who will surge forward at the slightest movement of your fingers on the reins, so his idea of tapping her with a whip, stopping when she made the right response, did not go down well. I could see she was clearly confused, not understanding what was being asked of her. All it did was build up her adrenaline, making her rush forwards. She would then be criticised for being disrespectful.

I will emphasise here that the trainer was always in perfect control of his emotions – he never appeared angry or frustrated, and there was a lot of understanding and compassion shown in other ways. I just felt, that like a lot of trainers, he had discovered a method which probably worked with the majority of horses, but he wasn't varying his approach with a horse that needed more sensitive handling. It is this "one method fits all" approach, which I just don't buy. For me, it is important that we really alter our energy and approach to accommodate the energy and sensitivity of the horse we are working with.

Being of an open mind, I recognise that all training methods have good things about them, and not so good things. Things are rarely black or white. At the end of the day, we should take away those things that work for us and let go of the things that don't. With this in mind, I did carry on with this training for about a year. Although Jazz was always tense and reactive in the lessons with the trainer, she was working beautifully with me at home. As such, it was always a case of just trying to learn the exercises in the lessons and then practise them much more effectively at home.

Exercises that she could carry out with her eyes closed at home were impossible to replicate in the arena with the trainer, so I finally decided to call it a day. Even though we were only having the lessons infrequently, it had reached the point where just the presence of this trainer was causing the adrenaline to flow, making her tense, reactive, and unable to engage the thinking part of her brain.

The experience had been valuable though. It highlighted to me that we still have a long way to go in the effective training of sensitive horses. Also, methods wrapped up to be holistic and natural can still be very forceful and intimidating. More importantly, I learned to trust my own judgement. This trainer had worked with some of the top natural horsemen in the world; his technical knowledge was outstanding. And there is no denying that he was carrying out some top-class work with the majority of horses – I witnessed horses going beautifully in bitless bridles. But he was not adjusting his approach to take account of my horse's nature and personality, and he was failing to see how confused she was. He was repeatedly telling me that my horse was disrespectful and not seeing me as a leader. But I knew this was not true. Apart from in lessons with him, my horse's behaviour and manners were impeccable. She has always tried so hard in everything I have asked her to do. As long as it is fair!

Once I packed in those lessons, I started working with someone whose views were very similar to mine; someone who was able to see things through the horse's perspective. For the first time, I had managed to find someone who Jazz was happy to work with. Our lessons were a big success, made more so by the fact that she was a rider biomechanics expert who was able to sort out my crookedness. Once my riding adjustments were addressed, then Jazz straightened up naturally. Funny that!

I have briefly touched on my training experiences here, but there are many others worth exploring. Thanks to the internet, they are far more accessible than in the olden days, when dominance over the horse was all that any of us knew. Thank goodness times are changing. Hopefully, the forceful and intimidating training methods will soon just be a distant memory!

# PROBLEMS THAT MAY HINDER TRAINING

## THE HORSE

### Physical

When we encounter problems with our horse, the first thing we are asked to consider is whether there are any physical issues. This is the right thing to do. If the horse is in pain, the only way he can communicate this is through his body language. I believe that a lot of horses suffer with pain issues, and they try to tell us through all manner of habits: aggression when tacking up, bucking, rearing, bolting, headshaking, tension etc. We need to recognise this is the only way our horse can tell us if he is in pain or uncomfortable. Instead of seeing this as naughty behaviour, we should realise it is the horse talking to us and that it is our job to listen.

Some horses are more adept at passing this information on. Jazz, very clearly lets me know if there is a problem, but Silver is much more resigned and will put up with things.

My advice to anyone who suspects their horse may be physically compromised is to carry out a bit of detective work. If there is a ridden problem, then lunge the horse in a cavesson and bridle to see if the problem goes away. Ride him bareback and build up from there, gradually building up the pieces of tack. If a change is noticed, then this can be passed on to the vet, helping him narrow the options. I have used this method successfully a few times to help get to the heart of an issue.

It can be very difficult at times to diagnose a problem, as a problem in one area of the body can negatively impact on other areas. For example, soreness in the mouth can lead to the horse hollowing his back, resulting in a sore back and neck. And once you get multiple problem areas, it can be harder to get to the source of the problem. You do have to be a Miss Marple at times to find what is wrong and where it originated from.

As well as the common mouth, back and leg problems, horses also have to contend with stomach ulcers, muscle problems, stiffness/arthritic conditions, suppleness issues and general crookedness. A lot of riders fail to appreciate that their horse's body is not that different to our own, in the sense that if you are going to do something particularly arduous, your horse's body does need to be sufficiently prepared for it.

Crookedness is a big problem for horses. All horses are asymmetrical and are naturally crooked, but it is more obvious in some horses than others. These horses are going to find schoolwork very difficult, and they try to relieve their discomfort through a variety of misbehaviours – tension, high-headedness, reluctance to move, running through transitions, lack of rhythm, falling onto or through shoulders, fighting the bit, or rushing. At worst they will buck, rear or bolt. At least through methods such as straightness training, we are developing a better understanding of how adversely these problems can affect the horse – not only physically, but also emotionally, mentally and spiritually.

It isn't just the big issues. We need to become more sensitive and tuned into our horses so we can pick up the subtle signs that our horse is not quite right. They don't have the luxury of being able to lie in the stable all day if they feel off colour. For us, a migraine can leave us reaching for the tablets and lying down in a darkened room, but for the horse there is no relief. We have days where we can barely function and would choose not to do anything active, but the horse does not have this choice. He may have to perform a One-Day Event on a day when he would just prefer to be quietly hanging out in his field. When you really stop and think, it seems a miracle that the horse doesn't protest more regularly and violently.

I also think we need to be a lot more mindful of some of the training techniques we adopt, as some can cause a lot of physical compromises to the horse. For example, in the last twenty years in the UK, there has been an obsession with getting the horse working "on the bit" or "in an outline." From the things I have witnessed over the years, this has caused untold pain and misery for horses, as they have been subject to being ridden in side reins or draw reins, or they have had riders pulling or sawing at their mouths; all attempts to get the horse rounding in his neck.

Any problem with the horse's mouth, neck or back is going to make it very difficult for the horse to work in a rounded shape, causing him considerable pain at having it forced on him. It is all a misconception anyway, because for a horse to be truly working in a softer outline, the energy should be coming through from the hind end and the back of the horse should be lifted. This can only be achieved through correct riding and the horse learning to work correctly over time. It is such a shame that riders become so fixated on this and I feel this thinking has damaged many a good horse.

## Emotional

If a horse is not in a good place emotionally, then he is going to find it very hard to work with you.

One of the common times that horses exhibit emotional insecurity is when they are taken on by a new owner. We have all heard the phrase, *"This is not the same horse I tried out."* Well, is it any wonder? He has been taken away from everything he is familiar with and ripped away from his family and friends (horses and people). The different surroundings, combined with new faces, are going to trigger the fight/flight instinct in a lot of horses, particularly those that are sensitive. Can anyone wonder why he is a different horse?

I moved Tiffany to a new yard when she was 19 years old. By that time, she had been with me for 11 years, so I knew her inside and out. The move did not sit well with her. For about a month she was a complete loon, cantering on the spot when I led her to the field, and was generally very fizzed up. If she had been a new horse, it would have been my belief that she had been doped when I tried her out. It revealed to me just how stressful a move can be to a horse, and we need to be really sensitive to this. They are not robots any more than we are. They are sensitive, feeling and heart-felt creatures, and their emotions can run every bit as deep as our own, if not deeper.

My advice to anyone who has acquired a new horse is to give them plenty of time to settle and accustom themselves to their new environment. In that time, you could work on establishing the bond rather than riding and working. In the long run, this will save you a lot of time.

There is a great natural trainer, Carolyn Resnick who, at the start of a new partnership between horse and human, encourages owners to take the 21-day chair challenge. Basically, in this time frame, she encourages people to just hang out with their horses, asking nothing of them. This helps the horse to gain trust in their new owner and to facilitate the bonding process. There is a bit more to it than just sitting in the field with them, but if you follow the daily exercises, which also includes meditation, she promises by the end of the three weeks you will have established such a good, strong bond that everything thereafter will just be a natural progression.

I have concentrated here on the emotional issues of a horse in a new home, as I feel this is something that we particularly tend to overlook. But any time that the horse is displaying emotional issues, he is going to be much harder to work with, as getting him to focus and concentrate will be particularly difficult. On these days, it is best to find something that your horse does enjoy, like a groom, scratching session, massage or just returning him to the field where you could just sit quietly with him. Again, we just need to be sensitive to how he is feeling and accept, that like us, he will have days where his emotions will run riot.

**Mental**

As with emotional problems, a lot of mental problems stem from physical issues or ill-fitting tack. But mental issues can also be caused by mistreatment, or inconsistent and poor handling. Again, mental issues can create problems in the way your horse works with you.

Jazz has always had a big hang up about cantering in the ménage. From day one, she has cantered beautifully out on rides, never showing any reluctance, but when asked to canter in the ménage, she has always expressed her anger – ears flat back against her head when transitioning into canter. There were times when I could feel she was downright furious. *How dare I ask her to canter!*

Luckily for me, she never did anything to express her fury, other than pin her ears back, but I was well aware of it. To start with, I just thought it was because she found it physically challenging. With head up, back hollow, and difficulty in keeping a consistent rhythm, it just seemed that it was requiring a bit too much effort on her part. Her difficulty in picking up the right lead canter exacerbated her annoyance. It was very clear that she understood what needed to be done, but she just couldn't physically achieve it. She would pick up the wrong lead, immediately come back to trot, and then pick up the correct lead – without me even asking. But as she became physically more able, with the ability to pick up the correct leg and maintain a good calm rhythm, her anger at being asked to canter didn't dissipate. It was also hard to maintain a good rhythmic trot after the canter, as she anticipated another canter transition. At times she would stop and refuse to move if she thought you were going to ask for canter. She has also expressed her displeasure if you asked for canter on the lunge; at times more vehemently, bucking, leaping and galloping for all she was worth.

In my attempts to understand her canter issues, I attempted to tune into her telepathically. In fact, a few years ago, I attended an animal communication course with someone on the yard and, as an exercise, we both tuned into her and asked why she disliked cantering in the ménage. Interestingly, we both picked up the same picture in our heads and felt the same emotions and feelings. In the vision, I was actually Jazz. My head was strapped down, and there was a man on my back. He was making me canter circles, but it was difficult, and my muscles were hurting. With my head strapped down, and my back and hocks disengaged, my front and back end didn't even feel connected. It was very hard physically to achieve what he was asking, and it was hurting. My anger was rising, and I felt furious. *How dare this man dominate me and work me so unfairly. Why do I have to be a slave to his ego?*

At least now, I understood that the canter issue was a mental one. Any request for canter in the school was triggering those feelings of anger, reminding Jazz of how enslaved she was to man's ambitions. So how to overcome it? For a long time, I left canter alone in the ménage, and concentrated on walk and trot. But eventually, the time felt right to conquer Jazz's demons. I wanted her to know that there was nothing to fear, and it was no big deal. On the lunge, she was mostly alright about it. Yes, she would pin her ears back going into it, but then she would happily transition between trot and canter. And it was a nice canter: calm, rhythmic and balanced.

Under saddle, I knew that things had to be done differently. She would anticipate it coming in trot, creating reluctance to move forwards. So, instead of asking for canter out of trot, I started asking it out of walk. In addition, I became very focused on my inner feelings. I wanted to flood her with good vibes. So, when asking her to go into canter, I would imagine we were running into the sea, flooding my body with feelings of joyful abandonment. Amazingly, this approach worked. Instantly, the resistances stopped, and there was no break in the rhythm of the trot afterwards. *"I can handle this,"* Jazz was telling me.

Now Jazz has no problems with canter at all, and she has a lovely canter. Her transitions are also very good. It has probably become her best pace.

This experience has proven to me how deep emotions can run in our horses. In a certain environment and asking for a specific thing where the horse has held deep emotions in that situation, they are replayed and those emotions once more rise to the surface. To combat this, we need to understand and see it from the horse's perspective. And we have to try and change the record, so we can create new, positive feelings for the horse in that situation. Once we start to re-write the story, helping the horse to associate with good feelings instead of bad, then things should hopefully improve.

I will always believe that mental issues can be overcome. The answer lies in patience, understanding and helping the horse to feel good about it.

## Spiritual

I have already devoted a chapter to the spiritual nature of horses, so I will only briefly touch on it here.

I believe that horses, like people, are on an evolutionary journey. They are here to expand their souls, in much the same way that we as humans are. But the majority of us don't recognise it. I am as guilty as anyone because it is only since I have been walking my spiritual path that it has entered my awareness. We completely overlook that our horses have things that they want to achieve. It isn't just about fulfilling our needs and desires; they also have an agenda of their own. Unfortunately, our failure to recognise this can make our horses lives very limited and unfulfilled.

I feel so fortunate that I was able to hear my horse. In doing so, and spending time sitting in her stable, she was able to channel this book through me, so helping to fulfil a vital role for her. But I am now only too aware that my own ambitions were shutting out hers, causing her to become sulky, grumpy, and unappreciated. How many other horses out there are feeling the same way; their talents and pathways blocked by humans who refuse to listen, unaware of anything but their own aims and ambitions?

The more enlightened instructors recognise the importance of retaining the spirit and soul of the horse. In so doing, the horse can enjoy his work and take value and pride in it. Instead of becoming shut down and mechanical, we see a horse full of vitality and joy. More importantly, a horse who has been allowed to express himself and maintain his spirit will always perform better and go that extra mile for his trainer. When your heart is in your work you are always going to give a better performance, and it puts you in the right frame of mind to learn quicker. The spiritual aspect of the horse is something we really need to acknowledge if our horses are to be fulfilled.

**Rider/Handler**

It is not just problems with the horse that can restrict his training. An awful lot has to do with the rider/handler. We have all seen those horses that have been problematic for one person but when taken on by someone else, they have bloomed and really come into their own. This can often be because their personalities just don't resonate with each other, and this does need to be considered. Personalities aside, I have listed below the traits I believe that a good trainer/rider needs to possess, if he/she is to become skilled in their profession. I will hold my hand up and admit I fall short on some of these qualities. As Jazz rightly points out, I am a healer not a trainer.

- To be open and flexible, accepting that every horse and rider is different. Each partnership requires a training method specifically tailored to their own strengths and weaknesses. Also, if something isn't working, you need to change what or how you are asking, recognising that the horse either doesn't understand or is finding it difficult.

- Have the ability to listen to what your horse is telling you. Your horse is always giving you information. Every twitch of the ear, swish of the tail and response through the body is telling you something. Your horse just wants to be heard. To truly hear your horse, you don't just use your mind and your brain. Use your gut and intuition to pick up messages that the horse may be sending you. What feelings are you picking up from your horse? Does he feel happy, sad or angry? Allow yourself to feel your horse's emotions. If you do, this can convey an awful lot of information to you.

- Empathy. It is important to think like the horse, seeing life through his eyes. Even people who have spent a lifetime around horses can find this hard. Not surprisingly, children seem to have much more natural empathy with a horse. It is not something learned, but something felt, and those open-hearted children find empathy comes naturally to them.

- Possess good internal energy. Horses are masters at reading our inner feelings and emotions, and they will not be fooled. To gain respect of the horse, you need to be able to control your inner emotions. Sensitive horses in particular, will become easily upset by your frustration or anger – they will just lose trust and confidence in you. Good self-control is essential if you are going to make any sort of headway with your horse. A rider who is mentally out of balance will negatively impact the horse, preventing him from accessing that calm place he needs to work from.

- Have good focus. When working with the horse, it is essential that your mind is 100% with them. There was a horse I used to exercise for someone. I quickly discovered that as long as I could keep my concentration and focus on him, he would behave beautifully. But as soon as I let my mind wander, he would be spooking all over the place. You are always going to achieve more if you can keep your mind on the job.

- Great visualisation skills. Elaine Coxon, one of the UK Straightness instructors, is always stressing the importance of picturing in your mind what you are trying to achieve. She goes as far as to say that visualisation should account for 80% of the aids and she does demonstrate this very well in the videos she puts out. A lot of top riders use visualisation skills to great effect when preparing for competitions. It is a shame that the rest of us aren't more aware of the efficacy of this skill.

- Good relaxation skills, including awareness of breathing. If you are tense, this will always transmit to the horse. It is important to breathe deeply, inhaling through the nose and out through the mouth. This will help make you calmer. We often have the tendency to hold our breath, particularly when we are stretching ourselves, but all this does is transfer tension to our horse. I am very aware of my breathing when riding Jazz and have found it can make a big difference to the way she goes.

- Great patience. It is important not to give yourself timed goals. There is nothing wrong with setting goals and having a vision – in fact this can be very helpful because you have set an intention and a picture in your head of where you want to get to. But as soon as you start fixating on time, you start putting pressure on yourself to achieve. All this does is create tension and disappointment if the goals aren't met in that timeframe. I have always accepted with my horses that it will take as long as it takes.

- Ability to be consistent. If the horse is to learn, then we need to make sure we are always consistent with our requests. There is a real art to this, and it is not easy. As an example, we may decide to release pressure on the horse as a reward. However, to do this effectively, we need to release every time, at the right time. If we are not consistent with this, the horse will just end up confused.

- Be clear and set boundaries. This is a very important aspect of training horses and can be a difficult thing to get right. All horses are different, and setting boundaries will vary from horse to horse. As with very small children, boundary setting is very important, as horses are masters at working out what they can get away with and where the weaknesses are in your training or handling. It is natural for any animal (humans included) to want to take the easy option, and horses are no exception. Given half a chance, some will try and take advantage. So, it is important to make clear what you will or will not tolerate. Setting boundaries gives the horse confidence as he knows where he stands.

- Control of the ego. This can be one of the biggest obstacles for the rider/handler to overcome, but to be truly effective in training a horse, it is very important not to let the ego run the show. We have all seen those riders who insist on the horse obeying every command and they will not let up, even though that horse may have a good reason for resisting. The problem is, by fighting the horse in this way, they are just giving the horse something to fight against, which often results in the horse resorting to bad behaviour. Sadly, I see this all too often and I feel it is one of the most important changes needed if we are to become a fairer partner to our horse.

- Confidence. The rider/handler needs to have confidence in their ability, because if not, the horse will pick this up very quickly. If it is an experienced horse then he may not be affected, but a more sensitive and more inexperienced horse will pick it up, likely losing his own confidence. One of my earliest lessons with my first pony Smokey taught me the truth of this. When it came to popping logs and jumps out on rides, I discovered very quickly that if I doubted his ability to jump it, then sure enough he would oblige and promptly stop in front of it. As long as I was confident, throwing my heart over the fence, then he wouldn't hesitate to jump it. At the end of the day, they draw their confidence from the rider, not the other way round.

- Have the ability to look at yourself honestly and critically. Are you riding well or are you crooked? Since owning Jazz, this is something that I have had to really take on board. I was trying to work on suppling her body when mine was hardly ideal. Try and look at yourself through the eyes of your horse. Imagine swapping places. How do you feel about the way you are being treated? Do you feel equal, or are you made to feel like a servant, your sole purpose being to appease your master? It can be hard to face up to our own imperfections, but I promise you, it makes a huge difference in the long run when you tackle your own weak areas.

- Don't resort to quick fix solutions. All problems can be overcome by taking the time to train and work with the horse. By not addressing the heart of the problem, you are only setting yourself up for worse problems in the future. Something I see very commonly are riders who decide their horse is too strong. They resort to riding him in a stronger bit. But if they worked at helping their horse lighten in front and taking more weight on his hindquarters, then this engagement would take him off his forehand. This will help him soften in the mouth.

- Be creative and imaginative. Try and expand your mind so you can think outside the box, and don't be afraid to try something different. In practising groundwork with Jazz, I discovered how responsive she was to my breath, and it didn't take long to teach her that two staccato breaths meant an upward transition. Once this was established, it was an effortless transition to carry this across to our riding, and it has made a huge difference to our upward transitions. Jazz always had a tendency to rush forwards into trot or canter, throwing up her head and hollowing her back, but the breath is so subtle that she now transitions beautifully with no tension.

- Be generous and praise your horse, particularly when he is doing the right thing, or he is focused and trying to do the right thing. I believe our horses really pick up on our feelings and thoughts, so try to make them good and positive.

- Finally, try to bring a sense of grace and joy into your training. I have discovered that Jazz works far better when I am in a joyful state (see the concluding chapter). By setting our hearts and souls free and connecting with joy, we pass these same feelings on to our horse, uplifting him in the process.

**Tack**

Another thing that can cause problems and hinder training is riding horses in badly fitted saddles or bridles. If the saddle does not fit the horse correctly, then there is a good chance that it will eventually cause a sore back. I really recommend when buying a saddle that you ensure it is properly fitted by a professional saddle fitter. It may be slightly more expensive to do this, but it is well worth it if you want to avoid the cost of back physiotherapy or vet fees. If the horse is riding fine bareback but displaying problems with a saddle, then you clearly know where the blame lies.

The horse also needs to be happy with the bit he is being ridden in. As horses all have such different types of mouths and different ways of going, then what is kind for one horse may be quite harsh and uncomfortable for another horse. These days there are so many different types of bits on the market that it can be a headache trying to find out which is the best one for your horse. I would really recommend getting out a professional bitter: someone who can examine your horse's mouth and watch them being ridden. From this they can deduce which bit may be suitable for your horse, and they can let you try out various ones they think would be the most appropriate. This is so worthwhile as it is important for your horse to be happy in his mouth. If he is not, then his work will suffer.

Your horse may prefer to ride bitless, and there are various good models on the market today. I ride Jazz in a Micklem bridle, which can be converted into a bitless option. I find that she rides very similar, whether ridden bitless or not, and she is equally happy with both. Silver finds it harder to turn when ridden bitless, so he is ridden with a bit – an option he is perfectly happy with.

**Feeding**

This is another big consideration, which can affect the way your horse behaves. Some horses are really sensitive to feed, becoming excitable and fizzy if fed too much cereal. Any feed adjustments should be made very slowly so you can monitor how it is affecting the behaviour of your horse.

The grass itself can make a big difference to the energy of the horse. The high sugar levels in the spring grass can make a lot of horses reactive and excitable. Other horses can become lazy and lethargic.

Tiffany was very excitable and fizzy in the winter months, and much quieter in the summer months, even though her routine and feeding remained the same. With her, the difference was so extreme that it was like owning two different horses. Jazz has been the opposite. She is quieter in the winter months, and full of energy in the spring and summer months. The grass does make her high as a kite, and those times when she freezes to the spot and appears scared always occur in the spring when the grass starts to make an appearance.

As is clear from this chapter, there are so many things to think about if we want our horses to be happy in their work and training. But it is worth taking the time to get everything right because when you do, your horse will reward you with a good working attitude. The most important thing to remember when riding or training is to have fun. It is supposed to be enjoyable, so make sure you make it so, not just for yourself, but for your horse also. If you are enjoying yourself and feeling happy, then your horse is almost certainly picking up these feelings too. This is a win-win situation for both of you and ultimately it will lead you both to a good place where you will enjoy each other's company.

**Keeping it Simple**

Finally, I have this to say: when I was a child, riding and training our horses seemed like an effortless process. We had minimal instruction, few riding arenas, and most of the training was done on the hoof. You had to develop a sense of feel, listen to the horse and rely on intuition to get anywhere. Even more importantly, you had to develop a really good bond with your horse if you were going to have any chance of catching him from the huge field he was kept in.

But these days, everything seems way more complicated. There are so many techniques and training methods that appear regularly on internet sites, yet some of these are described in terminology that just leaves your head spinning! This does make me wonder; have we become so dependent on instruction that we can't figure things out for ourselves? What happened to simplicity? Maybe, just maybe, we need to put aside our seriousness, our intensity, and just connect to horses through joy. Find the joy we experienced as children. For when we meet our horses in this Field of Dreams, we can really start to experience a magical union.

# Chapter 9 – The Sports/Competitive Horse

*You carried us to battle*
*No medals to show,*
*You laid down your life*
*At the hands of our foe,*
*In the blood drenched field*
*You galloped so brave,*
*Used energy and speed*
*Your rider to save.*

*Today we still harness*
*That power of flight,*
*On the racecourse proven*
*A creature of might.*
*Men's pockets you line*
*With silver and gold,*
*But where's your reward*
*For being so bold?*

*Man has tamed your spirit*
*Your urge to flee,*
*We have much to learn*
*From your humility.*

As you may have guessed, when I wrote this poem I was in quite a distressed state. It was following the Grand National, and a few horses had died on the track. My reaction was probably the same as a lot of horse-lovers all over the world: why does man have to sacrifice such a beautiful, majestic and willing animal in the name of sport? A sport that puts a vast sum of money into the pockets of the owners of winning racehorses, as well as all the other profiteers – trainers, betting shops, gamblers, to name but a few. Once again, we are faced with a situation where the horses' needs are put last behind the people who are exploiting his talents.

It isn't just the fact that many racehorses are dying or severely injured on the tracks; their lives in other ways can be quite unnatural. They are kept in stables, with no field turnout. This can be highly stressful for a horse who was designed to run free and travel for up to 100 miles a day. To cope with this level of stress, some of these horses adopt strategies such as weaving and crib-biting- bad habits that release endorphins into the brain, giving him some comfort at least. The only problem is that these repetitive habits can cause joint problems and digestive issues.

Then there is the widely reported fact that up to 90% of racehorses suffer from gastric ulcers: a painful condition of the stomach lining that is expensive and complicated to treat. Added to this, a lot of racehorses are still babies when they start their training; the fast pace they are worked and the pounding on the tracks can cause so many problems to immature bones and joints. Finally, when a racehorse is ready to retire (often when he is only about 5 years old), there aren't enough homes for these horses to go into or enough people who have the expertise to retrain them for something else. As a result, a lot of horses end up being slaughtered for meat.

It is for all these reasons that I have been particularly opposed to the racing industry. It isn't just racing either. I have always been concerned with how badly we use horses for our own ends, and it has always bothered me that horses at the top of their game (racing, eventing, dressage, show jumping), often lose their lives or suffer bad injuries just so they can appease the human ego.

However, I do realise the need to not get swept away by emotion and to take a balanced view. With this in mind, I decided to ask Jazz for her take on the situation. Her answer really surprised me and gave me food for thought. I have kept it in her words.

### Jazz's Perspective on Racehorses

*My dad was a very successful racehorse and he loved it. He was bred to race, and he had fantastic bloodlines. Being in his blood, he loved nothing better than the feeling of speed and the wind rushing by. He was good and he knew it, amassing more than £200,000 in prize money. He also held the record in the Italian Derby for 15 years. After his racing career ended, he was put to stud and sired a lot of very good quality foals. He was still getting placed in top quality stallion showing classes when he was in his twenties, proving that even when old he had maintained his beautiful condition. The racing had not taken a toll on him. Without doubt, he was one of the lucky ones, remaining appreciated and loved until the day he died.*

*It is important to take a balanced view. It may appear that quite a few horses are getting injured or losing their lives on the track, but this can be a misconception. When you consider the hundreds of thousands of horses that race, only a tiny proportion suffer a fatality on the track. Ask yourself this: how many horses lose their lives frolicking about in the fields? As a percentage, it is probably not very different.*

*Although horses don't have the same egos as humans, they do still like to compete against each other. This can take all sorts of forms: racing each other in the field (a particular popular pastime for young horses), pushing each other about (the equivalent of puppy play), and competing for the best hay/food/water/mate. So, horses do take pride in excelling at things.*

*When it comes to competition, a horse has to love doing it otherwise he would be no good at it. To succeed at any sport, unless your heart and soul is completely given over to it, you can forget it. This applies to all sports, not just racing. Those horses that don't enjoy it will be taken out of the sport pretty quickly (as I was with polo), as it would just be a waste of time and money to persevere. For top level competition, there are years of breeding that go into producing the right horse for the job. As a result, most horses that have undergone this careful genetic engineering are bred with the natural instinct to carry out the role. More than this, they desire to do that job, and some horses will become depressed if they are not fulfilling the potential for which they were bred. Like humans, horses will gladly give their lives for something they love.*

*For racehorses, there is a big purpose in what they do, and they have chosen to take on this role for a very important reason. This applies to all topflight horse sports, but particularly racing because this is the biggest horse event where there are more non-horsey people watching. When you see a horse in full flight, stretched out to his full capacity on the racetrack, you can't fail to be struck by his power, speed, beauty, courage, heart and humility. When you see a horse win from the front, or you witness a horse trailing who, on suddenly discovering his power and rhythm, goes storming past the rest of the field, you can't fail to be touched by his spirit.*

*Audiences who witness this, are united in their excitement and appreciation of those wonderful horses. More than anything, they are awestruck by an animal who seems to have sprouted wings. In feeling these emotions, they have been touched by the heart and soul of the horse. The racetrack is a great place to reach out to so many people; not just people who naturally love horses, but people who normally have nothing to do with them and know very little about them. The sheer magnificence of the horse is brought onto the stage for millions to witness. At an unconscious level, a seed of awareness is being sown into the mind of every person who has been witness to the power and majesty of the horse. Eventually, that awareness will lead man onto a more progressive evolutionary path.*

*In the same way that spectators are bewitched by the speed and power of the horse, most of the audience will also feel the pain of a horse dying on the track. They will be united in grief. That moment also raises a question in everyone's mind, "Is this right? Do we have the right to do this to such a beautiful animal; an animal that is giving his heart and soul for our entertainment?" Possibly at this moment in time, not enough people are thinking this way. But one day, if man evolves the way he is expected, they will. A time will come when people will consider what is fair and best for the horse and the selfishness of man will be put to one side. Horses will continue to race, and so they should. They are fulfilling their destiny and man is witnessing a beautiful spectacle. But it will be made safer and fairer. It will become less about exploitation and more about glorification of the horse; he will be fully appreciated, revered and seen as an equal. The racetrack will become a place where the perfect partnership between man and horse is exalted and witnessed.*

*I have concentrated on racing because it is in my blood, but the same thinking also applies to other sports such as eventing, dressage and show jumping. The cross-country course in particular showcases the unbelievable bravery, courage and heart that the rider/horse partnership possesses to even attempt to clear those jumps. The average person walks the course of a 4\* event with absolute incredulity. How brave must the horses be to attempt such a feat? Again, the horse has to possess incredible willpower and the ability to really attack those fences. The horse and rider must have complete trust and faith in each other if they are to stand any chance of getting around those huge courses in one piece. Most people are humbled and awestruck by the willingness and majesty of an animal that can take such a feat on; not only for himself, but for the rider on his back. When you really stop and think about it, miraculous is the only word to describe it. The partnership is so finely tuned, that even the smallest lack of focus or slightest error in judgement can be catastrophic for both horse and rider – their very lives can hang in the balance. As with racing, the true wonder of the horse is evident to the people spectating at these events. Is there anything that the horse is unwilling to do to prove his love for you humans?*

## I Reflect

Jazz has helped me to balance my thinking. I realise now that I had ventured into an emotional minefield, where my concerns for the welfare of the horse were distorting the truth. It is easy to become so protective that we become smothering, suffocating the brilliance and natural athleticism of the horse in the process.

It is a great point that horses will only do what they love doing. Just this morning, as I hacked Jazz out, I was reminded of a pony at a local show. His rider had fallen off, but the pony continued the round on his own, jumping all the jumps. After about ten jumps, someone managed to catch him and take him out the ring. That pony clearly loved his job and was choosing to do it, rider or no rider. As I thought about this incident, which occurred about thirty years ago, I did acknowledge that it was very unusual, as I have not witnessed it since. That is, until this afternoon. As I glanced at my Facebook page, I happened to see a video of a rider jumping around a four-foot set of jumps at an indoor competition. She fell off quite early on in the round, but the horse continued to jump happily around the course, clearing at least twenty fences before he was caught.

I never cease to be amazed by synchronicity, and my spiritual journey has taught me there are no such things as coincidence. Once again, the Universe is obliging, by showing me that some horses really do enjoy their jobs. What I witnessed thirty years ago wasn't just a one-off wonder. There are other horses who are just as passionate about fulfilling their purpose and doing what they love.

This chapter for me has been important. I am reminded of the need to keep a balanced view and to see it from all sides. Yes, we do need to always work on the safety and fairness for the horse, but at the same time we need to be careful that we do not suffocate the horses' natural athleticism, courage and majesty, reducing him to the equivalent of a stuffed toy.

The horse's power, speed and beauty needs to be kept alive for all to see and witness. Only then can we protect the purest bloodlines, ensuring the future horse is graced on a stage that is fit for his purpose. On that stage, we can all come to recognise the sheer miracle of the horse, displayed in all his glory. It is a way that the horse can reach out and touch every one of us – not just natural horse lovers, but everyone. And through that witness, our hearts will be subjugated to opening that little bit wider.

# Chapter 10 – The Psychic Horse

*Just because you can't see something*
*Does not mean it doesn't exist.*
*God gave the horse wings to fly.*
*When I am on the back of a horse in full flight,*
*I know it is true.*

Jazz made it very clear that I was to include a chapter on the psychic ability of the horse. She feels it is an underrated sense in the horse, and that if we understood how strong an ability this was, we could learn to work with it far more than we do. The horse finds it very easy to pick up on our thoughts, mood and energy, and so when we are around horses, we need to be a lot more conscious of what we are conveying to this intuitive animal.

It is reckoned that all of us have a sixth sense and psychic ability. But because our society doesn't recognise this, like an untrained muscle, it becomes wasted. This doesn't mean to say that it can't be resurrected. When you recognise it as a natural ability and start using it, then like any wasted muscle, it becomes toned and useful again. As with any of the senses, the sixth sense is definitely stronger and more developed in some people than others.

Exactly the same rules apply to horses. I do believe that the horses' sixth sense and psychic skills are generally stronger than in humans, but as with humans, they are a lot stronger in some horses than others. It is starting to become more and more recognised, and a lot of the modern training methods that I am drawn to acknowledge and use the telepathic ability between man and horse very much. The rider's ability to see the "inner picture" of what they are trying to achieve and sharing this picture with the horse is regarded by some trainers as more important than applying aids. With my own horse Jazz, I am currently attributing our recent improvements down to the energy in my body and the pictures I am sending her.

I first became conscious of this ability in horses, when I read *"Talking with Horses"* by Henry Blake. This fascinating book was written by a Welsh farmer in the 1960's and it has been credited with being the forerunner to animal communication. This farmer discovered by accident that he had a seeming telepathic link with the animals on his farm. Those times he awoke in the night, he knew instinctively that something was wrong with one of the animals and he needed to check on them. Sure enough, he would find an animal that had been injured or taken ill. Through a series of very long experiments which he undertook over a period of about ten years, he satisfied himself and his wife that the telepathic link existed, not only between himself and the horses, but between close, bonded horses. Strangely enough (or not so strange, as the Universe always strives to prove things) as I was reading this book, I witnessed this for myself.

We had taken the horses on a fun-ride, and one of the girls we had travelled with had brought along her coloured pony, Popcorn. We were grazing the horses on a hill when Popcorn's head suddenly shot up and she started neighing. A long way away, a trailer had entered the gateway into the grounds and on that trailer was Popcorn's very close friend with whom she shared a field. We were all amazed. How on Earth had Popcorn known? We were so far away and there were so many horses around us that it seemed impossible that Popcorn could have detected this through scent alone. For me, it was proof of what I was reading in my book – bonded horses do share a psychic awareness.

After reading this book, it confirmed something to me. I had always believed that my horse Tiffany, who I had shared 26 years of my life was very psychic and that in many ways she had been able to share this ability with me. Now I felt certain. There were quite a few events over the years that led me to this conclusion.

**Tiffany's Psychic Abilities**

As I pointed out in chapter 5 (The Teaching Horse), Tiffany and I shared an incredible bond from day 1; a bond that pointed towards a soul-mate connection. This does make me wonder: was Tiffany's psychic ability down to the fact that we had a soul connection and so could read each other so easily, or was Tiffany actually a psychic horse? I guess I'll never really know the answer to this question.

Certainly, the first instance of Tiffany's extraordinary ability suggested the latter, as it had nothing to do with me. This was the incident with the bog, as told in chapter 5 (The Spiritual Horse). I do accept though that it is claimed that horses are able to detect bogs through their smell, so this may not have been a psychic ability. But even so, how would a horse who has been domesticated all her life, with no experience of bogs, even begin to understand the danger?

I was always amazed at Tiffany's talent to follow any instructions I gave her to the letter. I first became consciously aware of this a couple of years after she had entered my life. Tiffany was kept in a large field opposite the stable yard, along with a few other horses. My problem was getting her out the field. Although Tiffany was always very obliging to be caught – she would neigh and come galloping over at the sound of my call – the problem was getting her out through the gate when other horses were standing there. Being bottom of the pecking order, she just wouldn't want to come past them.

Even though I was totally oblivious to animal communication at this point, I decided to attempt the craziest method of all to extract my horse from the field. I calmly explained to her that I would distract the horses at the gate with treats, and she should take herself to a second gate that was about 50 feet away. I would then run down and open the gate, enabling her to walk into the yard and into her stable. Looking back, I can't even believe that I thought this would work. But work it did; and not just that once. From that moment on, this was my most used method of getting her out of that field. Every time it worked like a dream.

After that experience, I always talked to my horse, trusting that she understood. Another experience stands out where Tiffany obeyed my verbal instructions to the letter. We were in the midst of a very bad winter. The cold, snow and ice had been particularly bad, but, as Tiffany hated to be left in her stable during the day, we had put her out along with the other horses. One evening, as I was bringing her into her stable, she slipped on some ice, causing her to fall to the ground. Her attempts to get up were futile – she was just propelling herself along the icy surface. I urged her to sit still and not to attempt to get up. As soon as the words were out my mouth, she instantly became still. I quickly picked up some bags of sand and spread this around her. The whole time, I did this, not once did she attempt to move. As soon as I felt there was enough for her to get a footing, I told her she could now get up. Immediately and thankfully, she was back on her feet again, and in seconds she was happily eating her feed in the stable. Although I was very shaken with my head swimming with horrible thoughts of what could have happened, I felt absolute incredulity that my horse had shown such perfect understanding, being able to stay calm and override the natural instinct to get up immediately. Thankfully, she didn't show any signs of stiffness or soreness the next day, despite being in her thirties.

It wasn't just verbal instructions that Tiffany understood. It was very clear to me that she also had an innate ability to understand the unspoken. One winter, when she was in her thirties, I had badly torn my neck and shoulder muscles. I was in a great deal of pain for many weeks and was finding it very hard to lift my arms high enough to put headcollars and bridles on. But Tiffany just seemed to pick up on this, very obligingly putting her head really low to the ground so I could attempt this feat. Once again, I was amazed how my horse knew what to do to make it easier for me.

Tiffany loved being ridden. I think this was a time that she really soaked up the connection we had. It also makes me wonder whether this kept her going for as long as it did. Whenever I rode Tiffany, I would always be very conscious of the amazing horse she was, and in my head, I would be praising her and basking in our beautiful partnership. In her thirties, I would feel such gratitude that she was still as exciting to ride as when she was young, and I would still feel ecstasy at her beautiful canter. I would be telling her over and over that she was my perfect horse. I now believe that she was able to pick up on all these thoughts and feelings, the effect being to uplift her, making our rides together a joyous occasion for us both.

As well as Tiffany being able to share our love of riding, she also knew whether we were going on a short ride or a longer one. If short, she would jog from the off and the only time she would walk would be the last half mile home. If it was a longer ride however, she would walk sensibly right from the moment we set off, understanding that she needed to preserve her energy. I was always amazed at how she understood this because the first part of the route would be the same, so it wasn't like we were setting off in a different direction. There was only one way she could be picking this information up; the answer had to be telepathy.

Over the years, other things occurred, which pointed towards other psychic abilities. They weren't just limited to Tiffany either. I seemed to be sharing these abilities with her. The most notable, mainly because there were so many witnesses, involved a premonition. Tiffany was about twelve at the time, so she had been with me for about four years. Whilst at work, I suddenly started to have a really strong feeling of foreboding. As the day wore on, this feeling became more intense, growing into the strongest impression that something awful was going to happen to my horse. I told everyone I worked with of my fears, and I rushed out of work promptly at 5.00pm. Arriving home, I explained to my parents that my horse needed me, and I needed to get up there as soon as possible. Tea could wait.

The moment I arrived at the yard; I knew something was wrong. Tiffany didn't come galloping over. Instead, she was standing holding her foot up, which was pumping blood. Luckily, there was a PDSA lady on the yard at the time and she was able to bandage the foot to stem the bleeding. If I hadn't arrived when I did, my poor horse would have bled to death. Thank God for my intuition! It transpired that Tiffany had trodden on something in her field (despite an intensive search, we never found what), which had taken half her hoof away. According to the vet, she had been just 1mm away from being lame for life. Thankfully, a few months rest and my horse was as good as new!

How fitting that in my very last hours with Tiffany, I was witness to an incredible dream (see chapter 3) which to me held a very clear message: our souls would never be separated, and we would be bonded forever. In those last couple of hours of her life, as we were waiting for the vet to arrive, I was very conscious of the fact that here was a horse who understood exactly what was happening to her. She seemed to have a lucidity about her that was beyond normal animal understanding. In the huge neighs she gave to her friend and later to me, it was obvious she was saying goodbye. At one point, she made it very clear to me that she didn't want me to leave her. I was going to check to see if the vet had arrived, but Tiffany kept nickering to me, and with her head over my shoulder she was pulling me back. *"Please don't leave me"* she was beseeching. I conceded to my horse's request.

Finally, there was the sense that her mother had arrived to take her to Rainbow Bridge. As she wheeled in small circles, Tiffany was whinnying happily (her greeting sound). My heart broke at this point and the tears fell – there was no doubt I was saying goodbye to my beloved and special horse. Although I was absolutely heartbroken, on reflection I was able to draw a great deal of comfort from these final hours with my horse and I am so glad that everything happened the way it did. Throughout the ordeal, I never felt that my horse was suffering; a huge relief for me and something for which I am eternally grateful.

There has never been any doubt in my mind whatsoever that the bond I shared with Tiffany was outside the realms of ordinary and that there did seem to be a psychic underlay to our relationship. My interest in the psychic abilities of horses led me to a fascinating story, which I have decided to include in this book. The rest of this chapter is devoted to telling you about a horse with other-worldly abilities.

## Lady Wonder (1924-1957)

When I first read this story only a few years ago, I was absolutely amazed that it was the first time it had entered my awareness. For someone like me who is passionate about horses and who has a lifelong interest in the paranormal, it just seemed incredible that I hadn't heard this story before. And the story is absolutely mind-blowing. Whichever way you care to look at it, there is no denying this was one incredible horse; and her owner was clearly pretty extraordinary herself.

Lady Wonder was bought for Claudia Fonda when the filly was only a few weeks old. She was hand reared, developing a very close bond with her handler. Very early on, Claudia noticed that they only had to think about getting her out the field for her to come galloping over to them. Impressed by Lady's ability to perceive, Claudia began using children's blocks to teach her the alphabet. She quickly mastered letters and numbers, so her owner constructed a piano-sized contraption with a double row of keys. A touch of her muzzle on a lever would cause a tin card with a letter or number to pop up. Through that system, Lady was supposedly able to solve Maths problems and spell words, as well as foretelling things.

As the Fondas demonstrated the horse's abilities to friends and neighbours, Lady began to provide answers that she or her owners could not possibly have known. Her reputation as a psychic quickly spread and by 1928 the public had come to know her as Lady Wonder.

As early as 1927, people were queuing at the barn to consult Lady Wonder and to ask her questions. Her talents were put to daily use from noon until three and this continued for the next thirty years. An estimated 150,000 people paid $1 each to ask three questions. The old photographs which you can find on the internet are fascinating, as they depict the horse at work. On one picture, you can see the people queuing up outside the barn in Richmond, Virginia, with the name of the horse written in large lettering across the building. Outside, there is a sign advertising her services- *"Lady Wonder horse. Will spell, add, subtract, multiply, divide. Tells time. Answers questions."*

The horse made national news and she is described as the most famous non-racehorse in the world at the time. As her fame spread, then so did the multitude of scientists, parapsychologists, and psychologists turning up to test her. Some claimed that Claudia was using very subtle cues to direct the horse, but this doesn't explain how she picked winning racehorses, political victories, located oil wells, forecast the stock market, as well as finding missing children.

Despite some people being hugely sceptical, others were convinced of her psychic ability. Dr J B Rhine, a researcher from the Duke University, was one such person. In the winter of 1927, he carried out a weeklong study of the horse, which involved about 500 tests. He even blindfolded the horse as a means of ensuring that the horse was not picking up cues from Claudia. His published findings in the Journal of Abnormal and Social Psychology stated that Lady Wonder seemed to be using telepathy and possessed a degree of psychic power. He did conclude that she didn't possess independent thinking because she could only give a correct answer if someone else in the room knew the answer. However, this doesn't explain how she was able to successfully make predictions.

One psychologist, Thomas L. Garrett, had exposed many mind-reading and fortune-telling acts around the country during his career. Lady was an exception. She told him his dog Mickey was alive in Florida, even though Long Island kennel had informed him the dog had died. Despite there being a grave, it transpired that the kennel had sold the dog for a profit through its Florida branch. Garrett described Lady as a *"genuine phenomenon."*

Lady was also successful at finding missing children. The police would often pay to consult with her in these instances. In 1952, her talents were called upon to find a missing Massachusetts boy. When consulted, Lady spelled out "Pittsfield Water Wheel." This didn't exist, but the authorities wondered if the letters were supposed to be "Field and Wildewater pit" – a nearby abandoned quarry. They took the search there and found the missing boy's body.

A similar instance occurred in Illinois, when two missing boys were predicted by Lady to be in a river near their home. Though the river had been previously searched, the bodies were eventually found there several months later.

There are some really notable and convincing articles written about Lady Wonder. One of these is entitled *"The Mare Solved the Mystery"* by Frank Edwards. Frank was a news director of a television station. He asked friends to travel 175 miles to consult the horse regarding the missing case of three-year-old Ronnie Weitcamp. In the article, he describes them thus: *"They went reluctantly. They returned bewildered."* On 24/10/1955, Frank broadcast the strange story of Lady Wonder and the replies she had given to the questions about the missing child. The questions and answers are given below: -

| | |
|---|---|
| Do you know why we are here? | *Boy* |
| Do you know boy's name? | *Rone* |
| Is he dead or alive? | *Dead* |
| Was he kidnapped? | *No* |
| Will he be found? | *Yes* |
| Where? | *Hole* |

Is he more than ¼ mile from where he was last seen?

| | |
|---|---|
| | *Yes* |
| More than a mile? | *No* |
| What is near him? | *Elm* |
| What kind of soil? | *Sand* |
| When will he be found? | *December* |

Frank was the target for editorial ridicule from various newspapers, but he had the last laugh. For on the afternoon of December 4, two teenage boys found Ronnie's body. It was determined he hadn't been kidnapped and he had died of exposure shortly after he disappeared. The child's body was found in a thicket in a brushy gully or ravine in sandy soil about a mile from where he was last seen. The nearest tree was an elm about thirty feet from the body.

Frank admitted it was the strangest story he had ever reported in his 31 years of broadcasting. He had no doubt of Lady Wonder's amazing abilities.

I don't think anyone at the time really understood what was going on. Even now, all we can do is surmise. Claudia believed her horse's accomplishments were due to a combination of unusual intelligence and capacity for mind-reading. In the 1990's the Richmond Times Dispatch, which covered a lot of stories on Lady Wonder (you can download these for a small fee) interviewed a former neighbour of the Fondas. She believed it was Claudia who was the real psychic, and she was using telepathy to transfer this to her horse. This was borne out by Claudia always insisting on standing close to her horse while she was working.

Whatever the truth, from whichever angle you look at it, the story is extraordinary. Just to get a horse standing for three hours every day for thirty years, turning over numbers and letters at the request of strangers, is nothing short of miraculous. While at work, the horse always appeared to be very sleepy – an indication she was in a trance-like state. Only when the work was over would she resume her character as a tense, nervous offspring of a racehorse. The more sceptical will point towards the vast fortune Lady amassed for her owner, but how could a horse fool 150,000 people, plus the countless people who tested her ability. Even Richmond City Council were happy to acknowledge Lady's talents. When the city annexed the Fonda farm from Chesterfield County in 1942, it licensed Lady Wonder for $50 as *"an educated horse."* It is also very clear from the reports that Claudia adored her horse. It was widely reported that after Lady's death in 1957, her owner was never the same, dying herself two years later.

When I first read the story, it made me question just how many Lady Wonders there really are out there. I suspect quite a few. But as horses are not taught about numbers and letters, there is no way of knowing how many horses can foretell the future. One thing is for sure: we need to be a lot more aware and conscious of what we are thinking around our horses.

## Chapter 11 – The Abused Horse

*"Ignorance is bliss" they often say*
*But horses live to dread the day*
*When ignorance can maim or even kill*
*Leaving them powerless against Man's Will.*

*Man holds such power within his hands*
*Horses subjugated to his demands*
*The horses' prayer will always be*
*"Please keep the ignorant away from me."*

On 30/11/16, I awoke from a crystal-clear dream. Unusually for me, I remembered every aspect of the dream and something else was immediately apparent as I opened my eyes. I had been gifted this dream to include in my book. In fact, whilst eating breakfast and looking through the emails in my inbox, this was very much confirmed for me. My daily *"A Course in Miracles"* message for today was thus: *"The Holy Spirit is speaking through you. You have a message to pass on to the world."* If I doubted before, I didn't now!

In the dream, I was driving along a country road. I was just coming up to a bend in the road when to the right of me I observed a large house with its own fields and stables. There was a five-bar gate, separating the drive from the road. Tied to this gate was a 14.2hh (or thereabouts) piebald cob. I slowed down, virtually to a stop, to take in the situation. The horse was tied to the outside of the gate, and he was sideways on to the road. I was instantly struck by his beautiful condition. He had a beautifully groomed coat, thick silky feathers and he looked to be the ideal weight. All good! But then my attention was caught by something horrific. The horse's head was tied really tightly to the gate, so that his nose was practically touching it. When I followed my eyes down his body, I noticed that his one front leg (around the pastern) was also tied to the gate. This horse, standing sideways on, could literally not move. As I stared at him absolutely horrified, he looked at me, his gaze boring into my very soul. Very clearly, I heard the word "*Why?*"

Having stopped the car to take it all in, I knew there was no way I could just drive away. This horse needed help! I drove around the corner, managing to find somewhere to park. By the time I had made my way back to the horse, two elderly ladies who had been out walking had stopped and were on the phone to the RSPCA, requesting that someone come out and assess the situation. As I walked towards them, a woman from the house came out, taking the horse and releasing it out in a field. Having done so, she returned to talk with us. She was very friendly and approachable; there was nothing in her demeanour that pointed towards aggression or nastiness. Very calmly, she explained to the walkers that there was absolutely no reason for them to have called the RSPCA. She was very much an animal lover, and all their animals were extremely well-cared for. As she was talking, her daughter, a young girl about ten years old, was behind her playing with a ginger cat. There was also a dog wandering around. Like the horse, they both looked beautifully cared for and in superb condition.

I struck up a conversation with the horse owner, expressing my concern as to why he had been tied to the gate that way.

Her reply was very polite. *"He has been misbehaving all day long, so I needed to teach him a lesson. He needed punishing. I don't believe in smacking or hitting horses, so tying him to the gate and taking his movement away seemed like the best idea."*

Breathing deeply, I calmly explained that this was not the way to go about dealing with a perceived bad behaviour. *"Horses' brains are very different to our own"* I stated. *"What we perceive as bad behaviour, is seen very differently by the horse. They are just acting from instinct. It is us that label this instinctual behaviour as naughty, not them. Also, it is impossible for them to make the association between their bad behaviour and our punishment. To the horse, they are two completely separate things. All it does is make us humans appear cruel and uncompromising. We are something that can't be trusted. In punishing the horse this way, we will either break their beautiful spirit, leading to them becoming shut-down and dissociative, or they will become angry and want nothing more to do with humans."*

The woman shrugged and her reply left me feeling totally disheartened. *"Well, this is what we have always done, and I believe this is the right way. He needed to be taught a lesson."* I listened in disbelief, thinking *"Have you heard anything I have just said?"* At that point I awoke.

The importance and significance of the dream was not lost on me. I know that in many places of the world, this exact same scenario is being played out. And the thought of it just sickens and breaks my heart. There are way too many horses in the world that have become shut-down or un-cooperative due to unfair treatment from humans. Some horses become so angry and embittered that they become un-manageable, eventually leading to them being put down. In Linda Kohanov's great book, *"Riding Between the Worlds"*, she describes how she takes on such a horse.

Having had his legs tied together in the stable as a punishment, the horse had quite understandably become so angry and hateful of humans that he was considered dangerous and unstable. But Linda just couldn't walk away from this beautiful black Arabian stallion. Even though her own life was threatened, she bought him, refusing stubbornly to give up on him. Eventually, he was transformed, and Linda describes him as one of her greatest horse teachers.

Some forms of horse abuse are very evident. There can be no hiding physical neglect or deliberate cruelty, and in these instances, it is very easy to get the RSPCA involved. But the emotional abuse of the horse is still very prevalent, and it is much harder to deal with. Even very experienced horse people who love their horses, can still be subjecting their horse to physical or emotional abuse by believing that when he misbehaves that he needs to be taught a lesson. I have come across people who believe this and practise it. And like the woman in the dream, if you try and tactfully point out to them why it is not a good practice, they will just tell you that this is their way, and you should mind your own business.

But actually, when a horse is being mistreated, it is important that we are a voice for that horse. I always hope that by speaking calmly and as tactfully as possible to such people, it might give them food for thought, helping them to realise that a good bond with horses can only be forged through trust. Trust can only come about by the horse having a good association with their human caregiver.

I believe that a big part of the answer to the solution of the abused horse lies in education. As well as young people being taught to ride horses, they should also be taught to understand how the horse thinks and learns. It is so important to recognise that the horse's brain is not the same as our own, meaning that he views the world very differently. Even a very young child can make an association between their bad behaviour and a time out punishment such as standing in the naughty corner. But a horse can't. He is not even able to label his behaviour as naughty, much less make a connection between what he has done and our punishment. IN NO CIRCUMSTANCES WHATSOEVER SHOULD A HORSE BE TAUGHT A LESSON OR BE PUNISHED. All it does is ruin a good horse and jeopardise the bond you have with him.

In my dream I was left with the impression that the horse had escaped into another field – by jumping or running through a fence. Instead of blaming the horse, we should be looking at why he is doing it. There can be numerous reasons: the lure of better grass, companionship, boredom, excitement, or like my first pony who lived in a 60-acre field with his own herd, maybe it is for the sheer hell of it. Because he can! But we certainly shouldn't be punishing him for it. With Smokey, I would just calmly put him back into his field. It stopped when he became too old to fence hop.

A few years ago, I was in a bookshop looking for some books to buy for Christmas. At the time, *"War Horse"* was showing at the cinema and a book had been published entitled *"Warrior: The Real War Horse."* I picked it up and started to look through it. It was based on a true story, about a horse called Warrior – one of the few war horses who, in spite of being used the whole way through the First World War, not only managed to survive but also forged a successful racing career following the war. The book, which I was lucky enough to receive as a Christmas present, very much highlights the incredible bond between Warrior and his owner, General Jack Seely.

As I picked the book up in that bookshop, my terrible habit kicked in; I started reading a paragraph in the last chapter, which was very much a tribute to Warrior's fantastic, courageous and enduring spirit. The amazing bond he shared with his owner was credited to the fact that this horse had only ever been treated with the utmost respect and dignity. He had never known a cross word from anyone. His beautiful spirit had been recognised and nurtured. I also read that the horse had died aged 34 and unusually he had not only spent 26 years with his owner, but he had also been ridden for the same length of time.

As I read this, I was suddenly struck by the comparisons with my own horse, Tiffany. She was coming up to age 34 and we had been together and riding for 26 years. Like Warrior, she had never known a cross word either, the result being that she was the most amazing horse you could wish for. She would bust her heart and spirit to make me happy. These horses will always go that extra mile!

As I read and recognised these extraordinary similarities, I was also filled with a knowing; the time with my incredible horse was coming to an end. We were on countdown. As the tears coursed down my cheeks, I made a promise that our last few months together would be blissful. In the event, I had been given three months' notice; something for which I will be forever grateful.

My dream for the future is for all horses to be treated respectively and lovingly from the day they are born. So many times, I have heard the phrase *"That horse is so disrespectful"* but never have I heard the same phrase directed at the human. So, we label the horse disrespectful for pushing into us or pulling us in his enthusiasm to get to the field. But it is perfectly fine for us to pull and push the horse all over the place. Nobody raises an eyebrow at that!

We have been very much brainwashed into thinking this way. It is only when you disassociate yourself from this way of thinking, stand back and look at the bigger picture, that it becomes so clear that the human/horse bond is very one-sided and dysfunctional. The horses are pleading with us to change our ways and how we relate to them. Do we have the courage to look closely and honestly at our interactions with our horses? Do we have even greater courage to change our way of thinking and make the changes that are so desperately required?

The horses have never doubted it for a minute. They just wait patiently, knowing the day will come when man will be ready to partner them fairly and equally. And when we do, the bond between horse and man will be so magical that there will be no limit to what can be achieved. It will be the evolution of a superpower!

## Chapter 12 – The Social Horse

*The language of horses is simple:*
*Be true*
*Be humble*
*Forgive*
*Do not judge*
*Live for today.*
*It is the language of an enlightened soul.*

Horses are very much social animals. In the wild, when they are living at their most natural, they live in herds. They are not designed to live alone. As a prey animal, there is safety in numbers, and so living together in a group is what all horses desire.

From the moment a foal is born, he is learning to be a horse. But to learn how to be a horse, he needs to be in the company of other horses. Even in those first few days, his mother is teaching him the importance of manners. If he becomes too pushy or too demanding for milk, his mother will just walk away from him. Those early lessons in politeness are very important. He needs to learn that he only gets what he wants if he is polite and asks nicely. As he grows, other members of the herd will teach him similar lessons. Too much boisterousness or cheekiness will result in a swift nip on the bum. He will very firmly be put in his place. Through this interaction with the herd, he will very quickly learn the importance of manners and how to behave around other horses.

It is claimed that foals who are bottle fed and brought up by humans are more likely to be problematic as they get older. There is a higher chance of them becoming bolshy and demanding, as they haven't learned the rules of the herd. This is just one of the many benefits of growing up with other horses. Living in a herd also brings them security and mental balance.

We do not always fully appreciate the social bonds that are formed between horses and just how intense these can be. I find it fascinating to see how horses react so differently to each other and how some horses are favoured so much more than others. When I ask Jazz about this, she tells me that the way they form friendships is no different to us humans. Their personalities and characters predispose them to being attracted to some horses more than others; just in the same way that we resonate more with certain people.

**Jazz's Interactions with Other Horses**

The social interactions between horses are every bit as complex as the friendships between people. Just taking Jazz as an example, in the eight years she has been with me, I have observed the many different ways she reacts to the horses around her. I have devoted the next few paragraphs to exploring this.

When Jazz first came into my life, for about a year she shared a field with Lauren's pony, Chelsea. They virtually ignored each other, but not to the extent that Tiffany and Chelsea ignored each other. With them, it was like the other one didn't even exist. It always seemed quite strange, but I put it down to the fact that with her previous owner,

Chelsea had been kept on her own. This possibly made her so independent that she just lost the need to interact with other horses. As Tiffany had always been bottom of the pecking order, she also had a tendency to prefer her own company, with the exception of her good friend Tina who was in the adjoining field.

A year after Jazz was settled with us, Lauren outgrew Chelsea. She went on loan to a young girl in our village and Silver came to us on loan. He proved to be a real charmer, getting on brilliantly with most of the horses he came into contact with, so his relationship with Jazz was pretty well guaranteed. Jazz very quickly succumbed to his charms and a close friendship was forged, although it was very clear that Jazz wore the trousers. Despite being very bossy with him, we have also witnessed the more touching side to their relationship. Jazz became very protective of him in the days leading up to his laminitis attack (see the chapter on *The Healing Horse*), and there have been times when Silver has returned the favour.

One of the most beautiful things I witnessed between Jazz and Silver was following his return to the field after five days away at Pony Club camp. As he went galloping down the field, neighing to Jazz for all he was worth, Jazz who was grazing at the bottom of the field, responded in kind. She galloped up to meet him, also neighing furiously. They clashed in the middle of the field. All the scene needed was the music from *"Love Story."*

After five years together, they very much represented the married couple. Although seeming to ignore each other a lot of the time, every so often you caught glimpses of their close bond. We have witnessed Silver becoming very jealous of the attention Jazz has given to the geldings in the neighbouring field, even to the point where this very kind, easy-going pony has actually pinned his ears back and charged at his rivals (ok, this bravado was easier with the fence between them!).

As I write this, I have witnessed something which reveals how deep the bonds go between Jazz and Silver. Before Lauren started university, we had always brought Jazz and Silver in together. But now it is left to me to bring them both in. I do not have the dexterity like my daughter to bring the two of them in together, as there are three gates that have to be negotiated. So, I started off bringing Jazz in first and going back for Silver.

Last night when I went to catch them out the field, Jazz was standing some way away snorting, with head held very high – intensively staring at something in the distance. This usually means there is an unknown animal lurking in the back field, possibly a deer. As I put her headcollar on, she seemed pretty much oblivious to my presence, too busy searching for the scary monster out there.

As I attempted to lead her down the track towards the stables, she kept planting her feet, looking back worriedly at Silver. She was making it very clear that she really was not happy to leave him. I was getting the clear impression that she saw herself as Silver's protector and leaving him to face that monster alone was just not acceptable to her. Eventually, after quite a few stops, I managed to get her into her stable. She completely ignored her bucket of feed, and with her head over the stable door, she neighed frantically to Silver, while he neighed back. She was clearly warning him of danger, because when I arrived at the gate, the previously placid Silver, who had been completely unfazed by the lurking danger, had now transformed into a manic pony who was desperate to get away from the threat in the field. He was bouncing and rearing in the gateway and practically dragged me down the track, desperate to prove to Jazz that he was safe. As we entered the barn, Jazz instantly relaxed and started eating her tea.

The next night when I went to catch them, Jazz stood back, insisting that I took Silver first. He happily obliged, practically mugging me in his desire to be caught. When I returned to the field, Jazz was patiently waiting by the gate, completely unfazed by the fact that she was the only horse out. She walked in calmly, happy that her wishes had been heard. As we entered the barn, Silver whinnied very softly to her, clearly appreciative of her kind act in letting him come in first.

As the winter progressed, I discovered that half the time Jazz would ask to come in first and the rest of the time she would stand back and allow Silver to come in first. In this respect, she seemed to have a really good grasp for compromise. It is interesting that most people believe that only humans are able to demonstrate this level of empathy, compassion and compromise. A little rethink required here methinks.

Jazz's friendships with the other horses in the neighbouring fields are just as intriguing. With Esther there was a very quiet, companionable bond. Every afternoon they would stand together, side by side, a girly get-together very much in evidence. But throughout their close friendship, I never heard them whinny to each other. Jazz explains that she really respected Esther's wisdom. It was a meeting of minds!

When Esther was moved to another yard, Jazz found solace in a new friend. She ignored the cob gelding Billy, but her friendship with chestnut thoroughbred Rosie was very intense, bordering on hysterical at times. And out of all intimacies, it was definitely the most vocal. There was no saying which of them was worse; they would both neigh crazily to each other. When I ask Jazz what it is she likes about Rosie, she tells me that she soaks up Rosie's admiration and attention. Rosie makes it very clear that she is hugely attracted to Jazz (same sex attraction is just as likely in the animal kingdom). That said, I have witnessed Jazz walking away when Rosie starts to get too amorous with her.

Particularly interesting was Jazz's one day love affair with dun gelding Buddy on the other side of the fence. Having ignored him for the nine months he had been in the next-door field, she suddenly decided one day in early spring that, as there was no Silver to flirt with (he had gone on a fun ride), she would make a play for the two geldings in the adjoining field. Being in season, she used her womanly wiles to provoke Buddy's interest. An interest which became so overwhelming, it resulted in the electric fence being dismantled by a 500lb horse, rearing and landing on it. With no fence between them, Jazz slipped easily into Buddy's field, and the next few hours were happily spent glued to each other's side. Any attempts to catch them just resulted in them powering around the field at full gallop – side by side and stride to stride. Hours later when they were finally caught, Jazz was put back into her repaired field, and Buddy was placed in his stable, as more fencing in his field needed repairing; a consequence of the gelding who shared Buddy's field bringing it down after trying to escape their antics. Having had quite enough of them, he had attempted to jump the fence.

That evening when Buddy was returned to his field, they continued to neigh hysterically to each other. But the next day things returned to normal, and they have ignored each other since. When I ask Jazz about this interaction, she tells me it was a one-day stand. *"Completely hormonal and it meant nothing. We were just swept away by the moment and the opportunity. Nothing more and nothing less! It was great while it lasted – even though it was only for a few hours. It certainly filled the time while Silver was away."* As the saying goes, *"When the cat's away, the mice will play."*

In the final stages of editing this book, I have to include something I have recently witnessed, which I found incredibly moving. After a year of Jazz being alone in her field following Silver's return to his owner, I decided to move her to another yard, where she could enjoy the company of more horses. Although she had horses around her, there was a lot of movement on the yard, and frequently she would have no horses next to her in the adjoining fields. I didn't like this sociable horse being so isolated. So, a move to a yard with the company of other horses guaranteed became top of my wish list.

Finding something suitable within fifteen minutes of my house, the move was made. Jazz was placed in a field surrounded by other horses. After two hours on her own, we introduced a small, native pony into the same field. As we led her into the field, Jazz came trotting over, neighing her greeting. But as she came close, she suddenly backed off about 10 feet. The reason was immediately obvious to me – this empathic horse sensed this shy pony needed her space and wasn't to be intimidated. Having been bullied by other horses, this pony needed gentle introductions, and Jazz had immediately sensed this. Over the period of an hour, Jazz gently grazed by her side, gradually drawing closer. In no time at all they were the best of friends and grazing nose to nose. And a few months on, Jazz has been nothing but utterly gentle with her, showing none of the bossiness she sometimes adopted with Silver. Just like with people, interactions with different personalities can bring out the best in them. Or the worst!

As I watch these friendships being played out in front of me, I realise that their interactions are every bit as complex and intense as our human ones. There is a time for play, a time for love, and a time to just ignore each other. Best friends are joined at the hip one day, but more distant the next. Their relationships are very much like the rollercoaster rides that we humans take on. Like us, their feelings can run very deeply for each other. And this is something that we can really fail to appreciate. There needs to be more awareness of the impact that the death of a friend can cause, or the effects of a separation between close friends. These events can affect horses on a very deep level, leading to despondency, depression or anger. A lot is made of how elephants grieve for a herd member when they die, but the same is no less true of horses. I have been a witness to this on a couple of occasions.

**Grieving Horses**

My friend's horse Tina was in her early thirties. One morning, she had gone down in the field and was unable to get herself up. I sat with Tina until my friend and the vet arrived. The kindest option was to euthanise, and this was carried out quickly. Her friend and companion of the last eight years was the same horse who had kissed and licked me when I was grieving for the loss of my horse (see Chapter 1). Now it was Esther's turn to grieve. As soon as the vet stepped away from the lifeless body of her friend, Esther appeared, worried and anxious, desperately trying to nudge her friend back to life. Attempts to catch Esther were futile, so my friend wisely made the decision to leave her in the field for the next few hours, catching her before the truck arrived to take the body away. A few hours later, Esther was still standing vigil over her friend's lifeless body. And she still wouldn't let us catch her. Desperation started to take over – the truck would be arriving at any time to take the body away. We needed Esther out of that field.

In a moment of inspiration, I had a plan. Esther was a close friend of Jazz's. Perhaps we should catch Jazz and bring her over to Esther – using her as a diversion. The plan worked brilliantly. We caught and led Jazz over to Esther, who was momentarily distracted enough for us to be able to catch her. Esther was led into her stable. She immediately proceeded to drink nearly all the bucket of water we offered her. We sadly realised that she had spent so much time trying to entice her friend back to life, that she had completely ignored her own thirst and hunger. Her only thoughts had been for her dear friend.

Finally, I was able to return the favour that Esther had given to me when I was grieving for Tiffany. As she continued to put her head over the stable wall, searching and whinnying for her friend Tina, I decided that this grieving horse was in desperate need of some Reiki healing. She had healed me; now it was my turn to heal her. I spent the next hour giving her Reiki, returning the love, empathy and concern she had shown to me those few years previously. Thankfully, this had the desired effect. Esther stopped whinnying, becoming settled and calm. Thereafter, she adopted an attitude of acceptance. Outwardly, there were no more signs of grief.

Esther was one of the lucky ones. She managed to overcome her grief and loss, going onto continue her happy life. But other horses haven't been this lucky. I have come across such a horse.

Maud had been in an accident when she was fairly young, and her injuries put an end to her ridden career. But she found another purpose in life. She was a substitute mum to a two-year-old blind horse. Happily leading him around the field all day, she was very clearly devoted to him. Unfortunately, his blindness was becoming a worsening problem. He was struggling to cope being walked from the stable to the field every morning, and then back again on the evening. He was finding it more and more stressful. Eventually, his owner decided to have him euthanised, ending the fear that was dominating his life. But although this was done with the very best of intention, Maud just could not come to terms with it. Her sole purpose for living had just been taken away. She was unsettled in the field, continually pacing- an activity that was aggravating her leg injury. The only time she seemed more settled was in her stable. A year later, there was no change in Maud. I still recall her owner, trying to hand graze her outside the stable block. Maud had no interest in the grass. She would just stand and stare into the distance – looking for her "child", who had mysteriously disappeared out of her life.

Eventually, the time spent in the stable was having bad repercussions for Maud. Her muscles started to waste, and this, together with her lack of interest in life, resulted in her owner making the decision to euthanise. Although a very hard decision, it was the right one, allowing her to be reunited with her beloved child.

Once again, I was witness to the intense bonds that horses form, and the breaking of heart and spirit when one of a pair is taken away. How can some people still refuse to accept that horses are sentient beings with thoughts and emotions that aren't so different to our own?

**A Change in Attitude**

As an animal communicator, I have become increasingly aware of how impactful changing homes and moving yards can have on a horse.

Just think about it a minute. You and I are very much sailors of our own ship. We can shape our destiny; the dreams we have can be brought into our reality. We have the luxury of being able to plan and map our future. But horses do not have this. They have no choice in anything. Everything is orchestrated for them. And a lot of horses are passed from pillar to post. It is not uncommon for horses to have numerous homes throughout their life. When you really stop and think about it, this must be absolutely horrendous for them. To have no control over anything; to not be able to do the things you want, or to be with the companions you choose. It must be so hard for horses to feel safe and secure.

When Jazz came into my life, I had an animal communication carried out, as well as some Reiki healing. Both the people who carried them out said the exact same thing. Although happy that she had been taken on by someone knowledgeable and compassionate, who only had her best interests at heart, she was harbouring a great deal of insecurity. Would she be sold on again?

I have found that with every horse that has come into my life, the longer I have spent with them, the more their security and confidence increases, and their true character starts to come through. It is like they start to breathe and relax. When I first had Jazz, it felt like she was treading on eggshells. She seemed very anxious to please and to do the right thing, but she was also very tense and at times seemed quite stressed and fearful. But these days it is rare to see her stressed or upset about anything. She has developed real confidence and with that confidence, she has grown into her own skin. Nowadays she is completely comfortable about expressing herself, knowing that there will be no punishment or admonishment for doing so. I know that her previous owner was very kind and understanding, but I guess the same understanding wouldn't have been shown on the polo yard or the schooling yard she went to. Now though, if she feels grumpy and she wants to express that grumpiness, it is fine. It is all information for how she is feeling in that particular moment, and I can work with that information. Being able to express themselves in this way is a really positive thing and should be encouraged. It is clear proof that they are not withdrawn or closed down.

As with humans, all horses are different, and some are much better at dealing with insecurity than others. Whereas a lot of horses will just accept their lot with a shrug of the shoulder, a more sensitive horse can be really affected by it, becoming anxious, fearful, depressed or angry. And can you really blame them? We need to become a lot more appreciative of what we are putting our horses through. There needs to be far more understanding and compassion. When we take a new horse on, there needs to be recognition that the horse will need weeks, if not months to fully settle in. Torn away from his friends and everything he is familiar with; this will affect him. In some instances, he will appear to come across as a very different horse that was tried out in his familiar environment. I have come across quite a few people who have bought a horse, only to claim in the first few days of owning him that he is not the same horse as the one they tried out. Some have claimed that the horse must have been doped. There is no thought as to how frightened and insecure the horse might be feeling, particularly if he has never moved home before. In a lot of these instances, the horse was returned. But all he may have needed was time and patience to allow him to settle.

## Weaning

When you understand the horse's depth of feeling and emotions, then you can begin to comprehend how horrific the weaning process is for mother and foal.

When Jazz told her life story (Chapter 4), she described the pain she felt at being separated from her mother. In some respects, she was luckier than a lot of horses. Being born on a stud and remaining there for the early years of her life, even though physically separated from her mum, she was at least aware of her mother's presence, as was her mother aware of hers. For a lot of horses, the process is a lot more brutal. I can't even begin to imagine the pain and anguish. I know how I would have felt if my babies had been taken from me at six months old. It doesn't even bear thinking about. Not knowing where they had gone and whether they were ok. A few horses I have communicated with have mentioned that the weaning was way too brutal and too early. They have never really got over it. At some level, the deep emotional scars have stayed with them. Years later, this buried pain can resurface, either as anger, depression or physical issues.

I think that weaning at six months old is way too early. Just because something has always been done at a certain time and done in a certain way, it doesn't make it right. We need to change our attitude, becoming a lot more compassionate and understanding. It is more important to do what is right for the horse. This should always take precedence over profit. For a lot of horses, the first touch of a human hand is when they are taken away from their mother. It is their first experience and contact with humans. It is not a good one, and it is no wonder that many horses are so deeply distrustful of us.

I hope that this chapter has demonstrated just how deeply the horses' emotions run. Like us, they are sentient beings and are just as affected by their feelings and emotions as we are. They can be very affected by losing a loved one – in much the same way as we can. By recognising this, we can take steps to help them. Through the work I do, it has become very clear that Reiki healing and Animal Communication are fantastic tools for helping horses with their emotional/mental states. It helps them release pain and deep wounds that they have been holding on to. And it helps us connect to them on a much deeper level.

## Chapter 13 – The Healing Horse

*Fulfilment doesn't lie amongst the medals and trophies you have won.*
*It arises when you look into your horse's eyes and feel the beautiful, shared connection.*
*In these moments you recognise you have won a greater prize; the heart of a horse.*

I have lost count of the times that people have said, *"If it wasn't for my horse, I just couldn't keep going. They help me get out the house and give my life purpose."* I have encountered a lot of people who are suffering/have suffered with depression, anxiety and panic attacks. For these people, their horse has been a lifeline. Horses, with their ability to accept us for who we are, forgiving us and never judging, offer a much more viable alternative than reaching for the medicine cabinet.

It has been scientifically proven that all animals have a healing potential. Most people are aware of the data that has been produced which demonstrates the huge benefits of having animals in your life. A study published in 1980 found that heart attack patients who owned pets lived longer than those who didn't. Other studies have pointed towards the lowering of blood pressure and reducing stress levels, through the release of the hormone oxytocin. Added to this, walking dogs and riding horses makes us fitter.

Animals can also keep loneliness at bay and help us recover from depression.

A lot of roles have been specifically created for the horse in modern times, all which are geared towards helping people in some way. These roles have taken the horse beyond his previous uses of carrying people, pulling carts etc.

**Riding for the Disabled**

The physical benefits of being around horses are not in dispute. Riding is seen as a good form of exercise because so many different muscles are used, as well as aiding with good core stability, balance and suppleness, so it is necessary for riding to be performed well. Riding for the disabled has really grown in popularity and this has had massive benefits for the physically impaired.

The benefits of riding, for those people who were physically restricted in some way, were only really recognised in the twentieth century. The achievements of Lis Hartel of Denmark are generally regarded as the impetus for the formation of therapeutic horseback riding centres throughout Europe. Polio had impaired Hartel's mobility, but not her spirit. In 1952 she won the silver medal for individual dressage during the Helsinki Olympics. The attention of medical and equine professionals was piqued and very soon centres for therapeutic horseback riding began to form throughout the UK and Europe.

In the UK in the 1950's, children disabled by polio were offered riding. In addition, a team of horses and ponies were used to offer riding to a local orthopaedic hospital. The RDA (Riding for the Disabled Association) came into being in 1969. Although originally formed in the UK, the vision spread throughout the world and RDA centres now operate in over 45 countries. The RDA currently supports 26,500 adults and children, providing riding, carriage driving and vaulting. From simple beginnings, the organisation has progressed in sophistication, benefitting hugely from the advice, training and guidance given by specialist physiotherapists, where planning and treatment programmes are developed for children and adults.

For those individuals who ride at a RDA centre, the benefits are numerous. When riding a horse, they are able to have an experience which is equal to the able-bodied. But the benefits go beyond the physical. They are also interacting with a beautiful soul, and like the rest of us, they are no doubt enriched by the rewards this connection brings them.

Disabled riding has proven particularly successful in the UK, and the endless medals we win in the equestrian events in the Para-Olympics is proof of this.

**Equine Therapy for Autistic Children**

Being around horses has also been of huge benefit to autistic children. This was very much highlighted in Rupert Isaacson's book *"The Horse Boy"*, which tells the story of Rupert's son, Rowan, who was diagnosed with severe autism in 2004. This young boy was unable to speak and was prone to huge screaming tantrums that would last hours. But around the horses, he was transformed. He became calm, more focused, and actually appeared to be connecting with the horses. And amazingly, Rupert noticed that the horses behaved very differently around this small, autistic child in contrast as to how they behaved around him. They appeared calmer and quieter, seeming to understand that they needed to be really gentle.

Recognising the huge benefits that the horses were having on his son, Rupert began riding one of the mares, with his son riding in front of him. This was when it became clear that not only was the horse's movement appearing to have a calming effect on the child, but a connection seemed to have formed between the boy and the horse. This was to such an extent that the boy started to speak for the first time – audibly- using words and sentences that made sense and could be understood.

Rupert took this healing one stage further. With his wife and son, he embarked on a two-day trip, riding on horses into Outer Mongolia. In this vast wilderness they spent time with Shamans, who were able to further his son's progress, helping him overcome some of the problems associated with autism.

Both of these approaches led to such improvement in Rowan that when they returned from Outer Mongolia, the Isaacson family set up The Horse Boy Foundation to help make horses, nature and kinetic learning available to other children, autistic or not, who might not otherwise have access to them. The Foundation helps treat children with ADD, ADHD, depression, anxiety, PTSD, chronic stress and more. Rupert and his team have built the Foundation in the UK to the point where more than 25,000 families in twenty countries are served on a weekly basis. Today, the Horse Boy Method and Movement method are regarded by many neuroscientists and educational scientists as representing the cutting edge in both brain development and education.

So why does riding benefit the autistic person? The answer lies in the motor, emotional and sensory sensations that come with riding a horse. Balance and spatial orientation are experienced through the vestibular sense organs. These are located inside the inner ear and are stimulated through direction change, incline and speed. Riding a horse helps liven these sensory preceptors, which helps make therapy exciting and motivates the child to be engaged. But in addition to this, are the advantages of connecting with a sentient animal, as well as spending time in nature; something which can be particularly beneficial to an autistic individual.

**Equine Facilitated Learning Centres**

Horses are among the best teachers and guides for personal growth and development. Being sensitive to the environment for their survival, horses respond to both positive and negative changes in posture, stance and breathing from other animals and people. Horses provide constant feedback through their whole body to incongruence between feelings and behaviours. This allows them to respond honestly and to be non-judgmental mirrors and teachers of our conscious and unconscious feelings and behaviours. Individuals learn how to use emotional, mental and physical cues within themselves and others to support their personal development. This creates an opportunity for profound healing in all aspects of their lives.

It is no surprise that with these qualities being more universally recognised today in the horse, more and more equine facilitated centres are opening. These centres concentrate on different aspects of the human condition. Some have opened to help teach leadership skills, others to help with behavioural problems, and others to help with psychiatric patients.

A few summers ago, Lauren (my daughter) and I visited a centre where the founder was a psychotherapist. The horses she used in her work had all been rescued. I was fascinated by the work she carried out and just how successful it was. It transpired that for a lot of people, this centre was the last resort. Everything else that these individuals had tried had failed, so by the time they arrived at this place, they were in desperate need of help. Amazingly, this lady boasted a 100% success rate and reckoned there wasn't a single person who hadn't benefitted. This seems incredible when you consider that the individuals who were referred had exhausted every other avenue. She described how her clients worked on the ground with the horses. Through the utilisation of various exercises, the horses were able to mirror the blocks and fears these people were experiencing. I was really struck by the calm, beautiful and peaceful energy that permeated from the building, the surroundings, the workers and of course, the horses. The energy was so incredible that it stayed with me for days afterwards. A truly remarkable place where healing was so evident.

Linda Kohanav opened such a centre (Eponaquest) in America. A fair few of her initial clients suffered addiction, abuse or post-traumatic stress disorder. Being around the horses created an immense healing space for them, where they could safely release their trauma and start to heal. She tells quite a few of their individual stories in her hugely successful book, *"Riding Between the Worlds."* The book makes it very clear how much horses dislike incongruity, sensing it a mile away. So, the person who arrives at the centre, laughing and smiling, suddenly finds that the horse they have chosen to work with wants nothing to do with them. That is until the client breaks down, revealing their authentic feelings and emotions. The horse that was so adept at sensing that the outer appearance didn't match the inner, now comes into its own. For once the person has revealed their true vulnerability, the horse is first on the scene to comfort and be present for them. Having asked them to acknowledge their problems, the horse now holds the healing space for them. For the people who arrive at this centre, it is nothing short of a transformative experience.

From its early beginnings, the Centre has now developed to offer varying programs and workshops, and it now attracts worldwide interest. Linda herself has written five books and is passionate about educating the world, her message being that the horse has so much to teach us; no other personal development tool can even come close.

**Equine Healing Centres**

When the horses connected with me after the death of Tiffany, I became privy to an incredible truth. The horses' ability to empathise with our pain and their ability to heal can operate on a very deep level indeed. Having been witness to this, it came as no surprise when I learned of a healing centre in Canada (Equinisity) that is quite unique; for it is not a place where people heal horses, but a place where the horses living as a herd, heal people.

There are quite a few videos on the internet which showcase this extraordinary place. There are beautiful demonstrations of people lying down in barns and fields with the horses, and of people being wheeled out on trolleys, the horses surrounding them in meditative contemplation. It is a place of calm and peaceful serenity, where all aims and ambitions are forgone, to be replaced by a beautiful sense of unity and oneness; a place where the human ego surrenders to the wisdom of the horse soul. Through that surrender, the humans are able to reconnect with nature and with their authentic self, leading to powerful emotional, mental and spiritual shifts as they raise their consciousness to a higher level. In this state, deep healing becomes commonplace, and lives are forever changed. It is no wonder that this centre is attracting worldwide interest, helped by the fact that one of their videos featuring the Centre, was the winner of the Equus International Film Festival in 2017.

Although this may seem ludicrous to a lot of people, I totally get this concept. After all, I have been privileged to have received my own healing; a healing that was so deep and profound that I am still not able to fully comprehend it. Based on my current knowledge and understanding, the only explanation I can come up with is possibly along the lines of this: unlike humans who live in their minds, horses live very much from their hearts. With their ability to regularly zone out of their physical environment, they are much more connected to Universal energy than are we. If people can allow their energy vibration to match that of the horse, then they are aligned to such an extent that the horse can be used as a conduit, in much the same way as a Reiki healer. In this state, the horse is allowing universal energy to flow through him to the person who has opened their heart centre. This allows healing to take place.

It is my belief that as we progress through this century, these centres will become increasingly popular, with more and more of them opening up.

### Jazz as Healer

In the Equinisity Centre, the horses live as closely to nature and their natural way of life as is possible. It would seem that in this thriving environment, their natural healing abilities are really allowed to come to the fore. It is highly likely that all horses have such capabilities, but perhaps in an unnatural environment these abilities are somewhat suppressed. Nevertheless, although rarer, the domesticated horses' healing talents are never totally obsolete.

Jazz has proven to me on a number of occasions that she has the empathic nature of a healer. Her role as protector has been highlighted in a few incidents.

On one such occasion, a horse was being clipped in his stable, about three or four stables away from Jazz. From the way he was fidgeting, it was clear he was not really enjoying it. The clipper's response to him moving around was to shout and smack him. I had just led Jazz into her stable for the night – it was to be her first night of coming in. Clearly, it was a bad night to pick. Jazz was most concerned about the horse being clipped. Each time he was smacked, Jazz would flinch as if it was her own body that was being violated. And every time this girl shouted at the horse; Jazz would neigh to him as if to reassure him. After ten minutes of this, I decided it was not a good night to bring her in, so I returned her to the field.

The most amazing witness to Jazz's empathic abilities, occurred in the spring of 2016. Jazz suddenly started to act very clingy around Silver. She refused to leave his side in the field, and any attempts to lead her away from Silver would result in her constantly stopping and turning around to neigh to him. This was extremely puzzling. She was not in season, and even when she was, she had never behaved in this way before – ever. Although close, they were both very independent of each other; there had never been a single instance where they had been clingy towards each other. It was a mystery!

The truth of this puzzling behaviour materialised on the fifth day. As I walked down the field, I noticed with mounting horror that Silver was unable to move. Feeling heat in his hooves as well as a digital pulse, I immediately suspected laminitis and rang the vet. Whilst we waited for the vet, Jazz stood with us in companionable silence, deeply concerned by her friend's inability to move.

When the vet arrived, my worst fears were confirmed. He did indeed have laminitis. This was such a shock, as he was a very fit pony and not in the least bit overweight, although later tests revealed he had Equine Metabolic Syndrome, giving him a predisposition to laminitis. As the vet injected Silver with enough painkiller to get him to his stable, Jazz wandered off. From that moment on, she reverted to "normal" again. Even though Silver had to be stabled for a few weeks, she continued to remain unconcerned, not even neighing once to him. It was like she was acknowledging that now his problem had been recognised and was being treated she didn't have to be his protector anymore.

This episode left me gobsmacked. There was absolutely no doubt in my mind that Jazz had picked up on very subtle signs that things weren't quite right, bringing out the protector in her. Yet we had been oblivious. Lauren had ridden him two days before his attack, not picking up on anything unusual or different about him. How on Earth did Jazz know? What had she picked up on? Once again it just proves that horses can pick up on things that are completely out of range for us humans.

It is not just horses that Jazz empathises with. This next story was recounted to me by one of the women on the yard. After finishing her horse one evening, she was feeling particularly down and depressed. As Jazz stood at the back of her stable, eating hay from the manger, this woman stood at her stable door, mentally asking for some healing.

The response was instant. Jazz immediately stopped eating her hay and approached the woman. With her head over the stable door, she started licking the woman's hands, proceeding to do this for the next ten minutes. By the end of this time, the woman reported feeling a lot calmer and more peaceful. She thanked Jazz for her help, at which point Jazz returned to her hay. When the woman told me this story, I was genuinely surprised. Although inquisitive, she is not normally a horse who will stand fussing over people for long. And she is definitely not a licker. There have been a couple of occasions when she has licked me on my hands, but this is normally when they are cold, and she is warming them up for me. This is not typical behaviour for her.

On another occasion, I was grazing Jazz in hand, when a lady on the yard came over to chat to us. She was visibly upset and was actually crying. Instantly, Jazz lost all interest in the grass, and directed all her attention to this lady. I asked her if she wanted to be left alone with Jazz for ten minutes, knowing that Jazz, with her healing presence could do more to help ease her pain than I could ever do with words.

When I returned ten minutes later, sure enough, Jazz had worked her magic. The lady smiled at me, thanking me for allowing them time together. She expressed her amazement and awe at how Jazz had just nuzzled into her, encouraging her upset to just dissolve. She now felt comforted, supported and understood by this horse who had so clearly wanted to help her. What a remedy to pain!

I don't believe for one minute that Jazz is unique in her ability to show empathy. In fact, as I am editing this chapter, one of the other horse's (Duke) on the yard showed concern over his ill friend. His owners were mucking out his field, not understanding why he kept neighing to his friend in a field about 100 feet away. His friend was also partially obscured by the 60-foot-long ménage and bank that was positioned between them, so he couldn't even see her that clearly. Someone went to fetch their horse in, only to discover Duke's friend rolling about in pain. She was actually suffering with a bad bout of colic. She was hurriedly brought into the stable and the vet called. Duke didn't stop neighing until he was also taken into his stable for the night. Someone very kindly agreed to swap stables so that Duke could be next to his friend and for the rest of the night he just watched her carefully through the bars of the stable, his empathic concern so much in evidence.

My hope is for this ability to become more widely recognised in horses, removing any doubt whatsoever that we are sharing the planet with beautiful, feeling and sentient beings who can not only pick up on our feelings and emotions, but who can respond and heal us. When this is recognised, it will hopefully create a shift in the way that people relate to these wonderful animals. A change in attitude and thinking is badly needed if we are to allow horses to fulfil their true potential.

# PART 3 – DEEPER CONNECTION

## Chapter 14 - The Human Attitude

*"......................and I whispered to the horse: trust no man in whose eye you don't see yourself reflected as an equal."*
*(Don Vincenzo Giobbe)*

In this final chapter, I want to consider the steps we can take to deepen the bond with our horses. This is not your typical horse instruction book. There are thousands of horse books out there which give advice on riding and how to take care of your horse. I want to take you beyond all that, and give you actions you can take which will help you connect to your horse on a much deeper level. Not only will it help you connect, but you will start to view life through your horse's eyes, helping to facilitate your understanding of how he thinks. At this deeper level, you will finally start to hear your horse and what he is telling you. And when your horse feels listened to, he is naturally going to be much more co-operative and easier to be around.

In Chapter 8, I set out the attributes which make a good rider/trainer. It stands to reason that if you are being a good rider and trainer to your horse, then you are naturally going to have a deeper bond, so there is some element of overlap here with the points I made in that earlier section. But it is worth reiterating and expanding on some of those points in this chapter too.

**Keep it Simple**

I have mentioned this before, but I do think it is worth emphasising again. Learning to deepen the bond with your horse does not have to be complicated. We can involve ourselves with all sorts of complicated methodology, but you only have to look at how successful children are at bonding with horses to recognise that you don't need years of experience and expertise. Perhaps we just need to adopt more childlike qualities such as love, joy, empathy and compassion.

**Open Heart**

Something that children possess which possibly gets closed off as they age is the open heart. When we are very young, love comes so naturally. Like horses, young children are far less judgemental than their older peers, finding it naturally easy to love those who are kind to them. Unfortunately, the knocks and setbacks in life cause us to close down our loving heart. We feel this action is necessary if we are to protect ourselves. But all it does is close us off, separating us not only from our fellow man, but also from nature and animals.

When the heart is open, it is much easier to be naturally sympathetic and compassionate. Unfortunately, our society brainwashes us into a more defensive way of thinking. Some people lose sight of the fact that horses are sentient beings, with feelings, emotions, hopes and dreams. These people become obsessed with their own ambitions, seeing the horse as just a means to their own fulfilment. They fail to take account of how unrealistic at times their plans are.

Time and time again, I witness people who are completely unfair with what they are asking the horse to do. Very often, they are just setting him up to fail. So, they will take their horse on a ten-mile fun ride, even though he has been standing in a stable or field for months on end. How would you like to be thrown into a ten-mile run with no training beforehand?

Needless to say, this results in horses being severely compromised, even losing their lives on occasion. A story was once related to me by a few people. The first fun ride of the season had resulted in five horses dying. The conditions were terrible – very muddy. Yet people were working very unfit horses at speed, with absolutely no thought to the impact this was having on them. This is completely unacceptable. It should be obvious that a horse who has had the winter off, needs to come back into work very slowly and progressively. Even schooling in the ménage can be very difficult for a horse that isn't accustomed to it. Asking a horse to perform circles correctly is no easy thing, and for muscles that aren't properly prepared it can be virtually impossible to do right.

When you open your heart around horses, the rewards are plentiful. I have always loved all horses, whether they are mine or not, and I have no doubt that the horses I have interacted with picked up on this. There have been occasions when I have been totally convinced.

A few years ago, there was a horse on the yard who had the reputation of being strong and hard mouthed. The trainer who was helping the owner, insisted on putting him in a

Dutch gag and riding him on the bottom ring, in order to gain some control over him. A few people on the yard rode him and they all said the same – *"Strong and heavy in the hands."* But when I rode him, to my amazement, he was nothing like I expected. I rode him five times, sometimes in the ménage, and other times I hacked him out, but every time he was the same – very, very light in the mouth. So much so, that I moved the reins on to the snaffle ring. I tried to give him every opportunity to be strong with me, by cantering him around open fields, but not once did he become strong or heavy in the hands. In fact, I felt he was the lightest horse on the bit I had ever ridden.

So why was he like this for me and not for anyone else? It was certainly not down to riding ability, as the other riders were all more proficient than me. Nor was it down to my hands. I had no lighter hands than any of the other riders. In fact, one of the riders who had been on his back, described him as the most hard-mouthed horse she had ever ridden. Yet this rider rode in a very similar way to me and her rein contact was the same as mine. There was only one thing I could put it down to- this horse knew how I felt about him.

There was something about this Gypsy cob that really got to me. Normally, I tend to gravitate towards thoroughbreds or finer boned animals as I love their sensitivity. But unusually for me, every time I saw this cob being led to or from the field, I just had an irresistible urge to throw my arms around him and give him a hug. I could sense he had a really big, beautiful heart. So, when I rode him, in my head I would be telling him that he was just fantastic, and I would be enveloping us both in joyful feelings. It seemed to me that on some level this horse understood how I felt and was responding to it the best way he knew how – by riding so beautifully for me. It struck me as incredible at the time, as this was in the days when I knew nothing about animal communication. Looking back now, it all makes so much more sense and highlights that getting the best out of a horse is far more than just being a good rider.

## Gratitude

One of the most powerful inner feelings is gratitude. There have been books written which are wholly devoted to this emotion. My own experience with gratitude has taught me how very powerful it is. When you pass this feeling onto your horse, he can't fail to be touched by it. It will certainly help with deepening the bond.

As a child, I spent every waking moment dreaming of the time I would own a pony. To say I was obsessed was an understatement; I could barely think of anything else. Unfortunately for me, my parents weren't as enthusiastic. It was made clear to me that my dream was out of bounds and having a horse would probably have to wait until I started work. Which when you are young, seems light years away! I can honestly say that I have never longed for anything as much in my life as I longed for a horse. Seeing people ride their horses would make me ache with longing.

So, when my dad did a complete U-turn, informing my sister and I that he would buy us a pony, I was beyond ecstatic. When you have spent your whole life dreaming and longing for something, on obtaining that dream, you really do appreciate it. There is no taking it for granted. I have written about Smokey in Chapter 6, *"The Teaching Horse,"* so I won't repeat myself. All I will say is, however difficult that first year with Smokey was, we never despaired of the situation we were in. There was many a time I would just stand there admiring him, not believing that we were the owners of this beautiful pony. Yes, in that first year, we may have found him difficult to catch, but we never lost sight of how extremely fortunate we were to be in this position. Not even for a moment would we have considered selling him or trading him in for a more compliant pony. We just felt incredibly lucky and grateful. And after that first year, when the bond and trust had been established, we really started to reap the rewards for being so patient.

I believe that if you carry the energy of appreciation and gratitude, your horse will feel it and in time he can't fail to be affected by it. How lovely for him to feel so valued and appreciated. Isn't this something we all wish for? You only have to think about how good you feel around people who feel this way towards you. Well, your horse feels the exact same thing and there is only one way it can go – to deepen and strengthen your bond.

For anyone out there who feels they need some work in the Gratitude Department, check out the book, *"The Magic"* by Rhonda Byrne. There are some fantastic exercises in this book and if you carry them out religiously for 28 days, you will really start to feel your heart open, allowing thankfulness and gratitude to flood in. Your life will change for the better, as will the relationship with your horse.

**Inner Emotions**

Those inner feelings can make a huge difference to the way our horse relates to us. Likewise, being in control of our emotions is vitally important, and this isn't taught nearly enough in the horse world. When you get angry with your horse and lose your temper, all it teaches him is that you are out of balance and can't be trusted. You are not a respected leader. The horse may be compliant, but he is being so out of fear rather than out of respect. Obedience out of fear is not a great thing. He will never go that extra mile for you, and he will not want to put himself out for you. Alongside this, your imbalance will affect him, raising his adrenaline and making him more unpredictable.

More and more experienced trainers are recognising that being a true horseman goes way beyond riding and knowledge skills. To really become a respected partner to your horse, inner mastery is essential. Until you have mastery over your own energy and emotions, then you can never truly engage in a harmonious partnership with your horse. Some of the best trainers are now recognising this and practising spiritual mindsets to achieve this aim.

As I have already pointed out, Jazz is incredibly sensitive to my energy. Sometimes, when I catch her from the field and lead her out and towards the yard, she will stop and pull grumpy faces. They are always the times when I am carrying stress or being defensive or hurried. I have also observed at these times that my breath is either very shallow or it is being held. So now I am a lot more mindful. As I walk towards the field to catch her, I try and think of all the good things she has brought into my life (including writing this book). This puts me into a state of gratitude. And hey presto! As if by magic, my horse walks in willingly, her ears pricked.

**Honesty**

As well as adopting a strong inner calm, horses also ask us to be honest with our feelings. They really dislike it when we try to hide our feelings or try to be something we are not. In their eyes, it makes us dishonest and something that can't be trusted. I have discussed this at length in chapter 5, so I only intend to just touch on it here.

Probably the biggest lie and something most of us have been guilty of at some point in our lives, is trying to appear more confident or knowledgeable than we really are. Outwardly projecting a great deal of bravado can cover up the fact that underneath you are scared rigid. You may fool the people around you, but never the horse. And he will act accordingly, probably unmasking the lie in the process.

**Good Listener**

To really develop a strong bond with your horse, it is essential that you become a good listener. This is something I feel we don't do nearly enough.

The truth is that in nearly every moment we spend with our horse, he is giving us information. And I don't mean the big, obvious things like bucking, rearing, or refusing to move. At all times, his feelings and opinions are being conveyed to us. For the most part, his conversation is very subtle: movement of the ears, a sigh, a snort, a snuffle, positioning of the body, swishing of the tail. But all of this is telling us something and it is conveying how he feels in the moment. A lot of problems with horses arise because they don't feel listened to. So, then they have to resort to speaking louder, or shouting. A lot of horses have to resort to bad behaviour to get their message across and to be heard.

Admittedly, each horse is different. There are so many horses who have given up trying to talk to people. These are normally placid, docile horses who, due to their extreme tolerance, will put up with the pain and discomfort they are feeling. Other horses become shut down and resigned, feeling there is no point trying to talk to people who refuse to listen. Some horses are naturally stoic or wanting to please to such an extent that they don't tell you until things get really bad. My last horse Tiffany, fell into this category. At 32, she suddenly started to catch her back toe on the ground as she was bringing it under her. The vet diagnosed arthritis. He reckoned she had probably had it for years, but her love of riding, her high adrenaline and her desperation to please had disguised it.

I am very grateful that Jazz gives me so much information. She has really taught me to be a good listener. This is one horse I won't have to worry about suffering silently, as she likes to give her opinion on just about everything. So that first trot or canter in the school is always met by pinned back ears. If her back is sore, she will pull faces if I come near her with the saddle. Luckily, we have never reached a point where she has had to shout loudly. I am so thankful she has never bucked, reared or bolted.

Since having Jazz in my life, my eyes have really opened up to the deep and profound messages that horses can pass onto us. I have already mentioned how Jazz's extreme grumpiness was her way of telling me that her life path ambitions were not being met. As soon as I started working on the book with her, all traces of grumpiness vanished. During a six-week break (weather too cold) of no book writing, Jazz had started to get grumpy again. But from the moment I picked up my pen and journal again on 1 February, all traces of grumpiness again vanished. It was clearly no coincidence!

More recently, when riding in the ménage, Jazz had started to perform quarters in when riding on the left rein at the point in the ménage when I was approaching the corners. As she wasn't doing it when my daughter rode her, I could see it was a clear sign to me that there was something going on in my body which was making it difficult for her to negotiate corners. For some years I had heard Jazz say to me *"Why are you always trying to work on my fitness, suppleness and agility, when your body is not in the best shape?"* I had chosen to ignore her for all the obvious reasons – too little time, too much effort etc. etc. But I now realised this was something I could ignore no longer. I had started to stiffen up, and some days just mounting into the saddle was feeling like a supreme effort. It wasn't helping my riding and it wasn't fair on Jazz.

I committed myself to an online rider training fitness program, which incorporated cardio, yoga and Pilates exercises. The results were remarkable. Six weeks later, the difference was really being felt in my riding. And not just felt but observed also. People were noticing and commenting. My left pelvis was no longer collapsing, and felt so much stronger and solid, making it much easier to support Jazz through left turns and circles. The best compliment of all was that Jazz was riding like a different horse. She was feeling so much straighter and happier, and in response to my stronger core, she was also starting to engage her own abdominal muscles. Best of all, her grumpy faces were something of a rarity. Nowadays, the feeling of harmonious riding is just magical. If only I had concentrated on my own flaws and imperfections earlier!

Once again, Jazz had delivered a very powerful lesson. We spend so much time concentrating on the improvements we can make on our horse that we fail to take a good, hard look at ourselves. We fail to see that our own unfit, inflexible and crooked bodies are severely restricting our horse's ability to work properly. This was a bitter lesson for me, as I recognised how much of a handicap I had been to my horse. Thank God for the forgiving nature of horses! From now on I am committed to attaining a better level of fitness and suppleness. I will be the partner my horse deserves.

## The Horse's Perspective

Seeing things from the horse's perspective is so important if we are going to truly understand him.

Let's just carry out an exercise here. You are the horse. Your Guardian is trying to load you onto a trailer. It is your first time. It looks quite scary. There is a ramp to navigate. You have never been up a ramp in your life, let alone stepped into a trailer. There are so many strange smells and sights. It is dark and you can't see. It is narrow and claustrophobic. You will be trapped, crammed into that tiny space. The floor is in the air and feels wobbly and strange – not that solid flooring you are used to. There are no other horses to be seen. What is this? Scared, you can only bring yourself to put your front feet on the ramp. Your feet are literally stuck to the floor. There is no way you can venture into the unknown. Your Guardian tries desperately to persuade you. She is pulling at your rope. No, you need more time to weigh it up and take it all in. Everything is moving too quickly. The next thing you know, other people have congregated. They stand behind you, waving their arms and tapping you with a whip. Your adrenaline starts to rise, and you feel even more scared. The more force applied, the greater the need to resist. You are stronger after all, and this is one instance when your strength can be of real use. You will not be forced to do something you don't want to do. Tempers start to rise, and being the prey animal you are, it all starts to feel threatening. Your fight/flight instinct takes over. There will be no loading today.

When you see life through your horse's eyes, things can look very different indeed. But we need to do this to fully appreciate what we are asking him to do. Although it may seem like an easy and insignificant thing to us, for the horse, with his more acute senses and sensitivities, it can be a very big ask indeed.

So how could it be done differently? I have to confess here that my horses are fine loaders, so it is not an issue I have had to deal with. But if I had a young horse who had never loaded, I would take it all very slowly, seeing the whole process very much through my horse's untrained eyes. I would make sure he had complete trust in me and his groundwork was good, or at least I could control his legs. There would be time spent letting him watch other horses load and unload. He would be allowed to sniff and explore the trailer in his own time, learning that there is absolutely nothing to fear. When completely relaxed about it, I would encourage one foot on the ramp, rewarding him for his effort. Gradually over time (weeks rather than days) he would be rewarded for making that extra step up the ramp. There should be no pressure – it is important that he has good associations with it, not bad. After all, this will stand him in good stead for the rest of his life. Something this important is not to be rushed.

Not long after typing this, I was asked to work with a horse on the yard who refused to load. He was being moved to a new yard, and his Guardians were anxious to overcome his fear of loading before the move in a month's time. A bad experience in the past, which resulted in him hanging over the breast bar, had resulted in his fear of the trailer. I will emphasise here that I had a very good bond with this horse, having used animal communication and reiki healing to overcome his fears of being clipped and lunged (he was averse to the lunging whip). So energetically and physically, I had already bonded strongly with this horse.

Well, even I was surprised by the trust this horse had in me. I wanted to take things slowly over the course of a week, as it seemed important for the horse to be happy and comfortable with every step of the process. So, on the first day, all I did was let him walk around the trailer sniffing it. Then the second day, I just asked for two feet on the ramp.

Amazingly, he actually offered to go into the trailer, and I had to hold him back. Although I was delighted by his enthusiasm, I also recognised that it was important not to rush things, as this could result in the horse frightening himself. By the end of the week, this horse was on the trailer, and was completely comfortable and happy with it.

The day of the move he just walked straight on the trailer and behaved like a pro. About six months later, he moved yards again, and even though he hadn't been on the trailer in the intervening period, he again loaded easily and effortlessly.

It was interesting, because around the same time, a woman whose horse I had carried out an animal communication with, had also asked for advice on her pony who was a difficult loader. So, I gave her a detailed account via email as to the steps I was taking, and she followed along and did the same thing with her pony. By the end of the week, her pony was also loading happily, and she had no further problems.

It just goes to show that taking the time to make our horses comfortable with things, saves massive time in the long run.

The biggest mistake I feel people make is that they just assume their horse will load first time. The time they ask their horse to load is when they are moving yards, going to a competition or going to veterinary hospital. In these stressful instances, the owner can't take no for an answer, and desperate measures are taken, creating bad associations in the horse's mind. Preparation is definitely the key here. Plan and think ahead. Give your horse plenty of time to get ready and to be able to meet you with confidence and enthusiasm.

## Giving the Horse Choices

Just recently, an interesting concept presented itself to me in an article I was reading. The statement that provoked a real aha moment for me was the fact that most of us desire a true partnership with our horse. But the truth is, very, very few people achieve it. Ask yourself this: how many riders let their horse make decisions for half of the time, or how many riders accept not getting their own way for half the time? My bet is that you can't think of any. For that is what a true partnership is- it is all about compromise. Reading through the article really brought home to me how much our thinking and attitude towards horses needs to change if we are to make any headway at all towards a true partnership.

The majority of people still think that horses aren't intelligent enough to make well informed decisions. But on the contrary, this is just not true, and studies have proven this. One such study which received a lot of attention was conducted in Norway in 2016, which demonstrated that horses were able to convey their preference for blanket-wearing, by signalling whether they wanted their rug to be put on, taken off or left unchanged. This was achieved by teaching them to touch one of three different visual symbols on white painted wooden display boards. It only took two weeks to successfully train all 23 horses to make their choice. The choices the horses made were very dependent on the weather. In nice weather, they chose to have no rug on and when it was wet, cold or windy, they chose a rug. This proved beyond a doubt that the horses could not only understand the consequences of their choice on their comfort, but they could quite easily learn the meaning of the symbols.

I believe that letting our horses make decisions for themselves is really beneficial. Not only does it activate and develop the thinking part of the brain, but they will have more respect towards us for allowing them these choices. Unlike us, horses have so few opportunities to make decisions in their lives. But the more they can learn to make decisions, understanding the outcome of those decisions, the more they will learn to work things out for themselves. As Mark Rashid points out in his brilliant horse books, this is the best way to train a horse. Given this freedom, the horse will very quickly learn what brings him comfort and what makes him uncomfortable, and through this learning he will be empowered to make better choices.

In Chapter 7 in the section on General Spookiness, I described a ride out with Jazz where I gave her the choice to go past some brightly coloured tents in a garden, or to turn around and take a longer route home. After a bit of indecision, she eventually made the right decision – plucking up the courage to go past the tents. I was pleased with how she had processed this and the valuable lesson she had learned: sometimes it is better to face up to your fears!

Whenever I turn Jazz out in her field, I give her the choice as to whether she wants to play some games with me, using carrots as a reward. We do simple manoeuvres like backing up, turn on the forehand, turn on the haunches and a good variety of carrot stretches. But it is always her choice whether we do this or not. If she chooses to, she will stay with me and either nuzzle me or go into her bow pose, saying *"Come on, let's get on with it."* She also has the choice to leave at any time. More times than not, she chooses to play, and when she does, it is normally her decision to see it through to the end. Having the choice is empowering for her.

Have a good think about how you can allow your horse more choice in his life. Drop the reins and let him decide which route you take; or let him decide the pace you ride at; if you have a choice over which fields or stables he goes in; or the companions he is to be kept with, then let him choose. He will love you for it!

## Hanging Out

Just hanging out with your horse, asking nothing of him, can be very beneficial in forging a close bond. Particularly when the horse hasn't been with you long- just getting to know each other can really help with facilitating trust and respect.

We all want our horses to be happy and comfortable in our company. If we only ever catch our horse to ride, or for blacksmith/teeth/vet visits, then he really doesn't have much incentive to be caught. Spend time with him, giving him what he wants – grooming, massage, scratches, rubs, Reiki etc. Anything that he enjoys and makes him feel good. In that respect, your horse can learn that humans aren't all about take, take, take. Perhaps you could take him out of the field and graze him on some better grass or some hedgerows. Whatever takes his fancy!

It is good to learn the value of the pregnant pause. Just talk to your horse, breathe with him; see if you can synchronise your breath. Meditate with him. And in the silence, listen out for the voice of your horse's soul.

# AFTERWORD

*Experiencing Joy in the moment,*
*Is enough to hold the horse in your embrace.*

It was a beautiful March morning, about a year after I had finished penning this book. As the sun's strands pierced their way through the sparse trees, a beautiful, golden light cast its net over Jazz and me as we played together in the school.

Although my spiritual journey and co-writing this book with Jazz has enabled me to gain a great deal of wisdom, like anyone else, I don't always practise what I preach, and I am prone to suffering temporary periods of amnesia. It is all too easy to sleepwalk through life; just going through the motions, not really connecting mindfully to the task in hand.

But today was different. Today I was mindful. I promised myself that whilst carrying out some liberty work with Jazz, I would really connect to the joy inside myself. After all, if I am just going through the motions, then I can hardly blame my horse for doing the same. During the last few days, I had been witness to some really beautiful events, resulting now in an effortless connection to the joy inside me.

As I released the beautiful energy from within, something magical happened. Unusually for Jazz, throughout the whole session she chose to stay connected with me. Normally, she will stay and work with me for bits of the session and the remainder of the time she will wander off.

This is fine. After all, this is what liberty work is all about – the choice of whether to stay or go. But today she was giving me a resounding *"Yes, let's play!"* She was doing it all – walk, trot, canter, backing up, turn on the forehand and turn on the haunches. And for the first time ever in canter, she was coming back to me. As we turned the corner to head down the 60-foot-long side, she cantered on alone, only to turn at the top, cantering back to my position, midway at the bottom of the school. Carrying out this manoeuvre a few times, I discovered to my delight that when she turned at the top, I could dictate her pace of walk, trot or canter, just by the energy I was carrying in my body. It was truly magical!

Finally, I finished the session by giving her the massage she loves, telling her how amazing she was, how immensely proud of her I was and how much I loved her. But I didn't just say the words. I felt them with every ounce of my being, speaking from my heart, allowing my love and gratitude to flow through. Jazz thanked me and told me she loved me back. How do I know? Because words just weren't necessary! Her eyes had softened and the love in them told me everything I needed to know. She proceeded to lick my hand, and lick, and lick, and lick..........

# THE UNIFICATION PRAYER

*Dear God of love*

*Please allow me to be the partner my horse deserves.*
*Expand my vision, so I can see beyond*
*The horse's beautiful form, into the purest of hearts.*
*Enhance my hearing, so I can catch my horse's soul*
*Speaking from his heart to mine.*
*Soften my voice, so the only sounds to emerge*
*Are the sweet notes of a gentle and loving caress.*
*Through the power of touch, let the light of love*
*Flow freely, reassuring my horse that all is well.*
*Free my mind, allowing it to merge with that of my horse,*
*Creating a dance so powerful, so harmonised*
*It is not possible to see*
*Where one body ends and one begins.*
*More than anything Dear Lord,*
*Please open my heart, so I can hold my friend*
*In an eternal embrace*
*Beyond time, beyond space*
*Forever unified.*

Amen

# EPILOGUE

It seems hard to comprehend that it was as long ago as 2016 when I started this book and 2017 when I typed it up. I was getting a very strong message from the Universe that it wasn't the right time to publish, and I needed to wait until I had set up my spiritual business. So that is what I did. Having just launched my business, I now know this is the time.

Jazz and I have both made giant steps forwards since that time and there have been big changes in both of us.

I am incredibly grateful to Jazz for encouraging me and even pushing me down the spiritual path, to the extent that I barely recognise myself from the person I was twelve years ago. But I too have helped Jazz, by being the channel through which she could express her voice; allowing her to achieve what she came here to do.

When I lost Tiffany, not for one moment did I imagine ever finding another horse with whom I could share a very close connected soul bond. It wasn't even on my agenda to find such a horse, as my belief was along the lines that such a horse only comes along once in a lifetime. I have been proven wrong. Yes, Jazz's lessons and gifts have been very different to those of Tiffany's, but they have been as equally valuable. Tiffany came into my life to help support my fragile ego, giving me joy and strength at a time when my life was very challenging. Jazz on the other hand, arrived in my life at the time of my spiritual awakening, encouraging me to pull away from the ego mind and the physical world, allowing me to discover my spiritual being and bringing me home to my true self. They are two very different times in my life, and each horse was there for me with their lessons and gifts, as I transverse the different levels of consciousness.

My soul connection with Jazz was validated a couple of years ago by an outside source. I work part-time, carrying out tax work in an accountancy firm, and one of my clients was so pleased with some work I had done for her that she sent thanks to me in her morning meditation. She recounted her surprise when she tried to visualise what I looked like, as instead of seeing a woman, she saw the face of a white horse, along with a lot of zzz's. *"I must be having an off day"* she explained, *"as this has never happened to me before."* I put her mind at rest by sending her a photo of Jazz's head (now nearly white) and telling her the story of how Jazz had channelled a book through me. Definitely not a typical day at the office!

Her observation made my day. This was a lady who knew absolutely nothing about me, and as she later confessed, she was taking quite a risk telling me this story, as to most people it would seem nothing short of bonkers. Instead, she was delighted that her intuition had been so spot on, and I was beyond happy that my connection with Jazz ran so deep.

Enough about me! How about Jazz?

Well, now that her soul purpose had been accomplished, for the next few years she gave everything of herself. My daughter attended clinics and competed with her in dressage, show-jumping and combined training. Even though I have no interest in competing, we did a dressage competition and jumping clinic together. In all of this, Jazz was amazing and didn't put a foot out of place. More importantly, she was happy and enjoying herself.

In 2021 Jazz contracted a virus, although pneumonia was suspected. After ten days in hospital, she was left with Atrial Fibrillation. Not wanting to put her through any risky procedures, the decision was made to retire her. Henceforth, she has continued to live her best life, sharing her field with my daughter's horse Rosie. They adore each other and along with their thoroughbred charmer of a friend Fred in the adjoining field, they have formed a loving threesome.

The outbursts of thoroughbred stress are much less evident these days. The last time Jazz became upset was six months ago when treacherous icy conditions resulted in the horses being confined to their stables for three days. When I arrived at the stables, Jazz's delight at my appearance was soon replaced by frustration that I was not going to relieve her of her captivity. Charging around the stable and threatening to come over the door, I quickly disengaged from her stress and directed Reiki energy to her over the stable door. Within minutes, Jazz had taken herself to the back of the stable and began releasing her tension through huge yawns. Although I have never done it before, I started to video her, hoping to capture her release. Well, I didn't catch any yawns, but what I did capture was something way more magical. For when I played back the two-minute video, there was no mistaking the hundreds of orbs flying around; orbs in all sizes and all colours, some moving slowly, others moving quickly, in different directions. The next day was a recurrence of the day before, and I was able to video another three minutes of orbs flying around. Once I disconnected from the Reiki energy, the orbs disappeared.

The full story of the orbs will be told in a future book. The most convincing evidence that the orbs represented nonphysical healing entities, was reflected in how well Jazz coped with the three days confinement. She remained completely calm and chilled throughout, like she had been sedated. When it was just about safe enough to put them out on the afternoon of the third day, she followed me gently to the field, letting me guide her very slowly and carefully to the field. Once there, she ignored Rosie's attempts to go crazy. While Rosie raced and bucked around the thawing icy field, Jazz quietly munched away on the haylage I put out. This was a Jazz I barely recognised!

It is claimed that orbs often make an appearance when healing is being undertaken, and they are connected to the consciousness of the healer. But who is the healer? I am not sure that I can take the credit.

For Jazz is still very much the healer. Recently, I was hand grazing her when a woman walked over to us. She was visibly upset and crying. Jazz immediately lifted her head from the grass and directed her attention towards this woman. "*I am here for you*" she was saying. In that moment, I knew that Jazz could do more to help this woman than I could, so I offered to leave them together for ten minutes. Sure enough, when I returned, Jazz had woven her magic. Tears gone, the woman met me with a smile, explaining how deeply touched she was by the concern and attentiveness Jazz had directed her way. By standing with her in silent awareness, she had delivered more healing than I could ever have done with words. Such is the power of a master healer!

So, what are my dreams for Jazz going forwards? My wish is for her to live out the rest of her life in peace and serenity, with absolutely nothing being asked of her. It is the least to ask of a horse who has given so much physically, emotionally and spiritually. Through this book, her soul and essence will live on, and she will perform the biggest healing of all - encouraging us all to move away from the still pervasive egocentric, dominating energy we inflict on our horses, into a higher consciousness, where we merge with the soul of our horse. When we reclaim the memories of our ancient wholeness, we will have found our way home.

If you wish to contact me, my details are…

Website: https://unitingsouls.co.uk

Facebook page: Uniting Souls through Animal Communication and Reiki Healing.

Email address: fiona.sutton@btinternet.com

**Jazz and me**

Printed in Great Britain
by Amazon